MznLnx

Missing Links Exam Preps

Exam Prep for

Management

Robbins & Coulter, 9th Edition

The MznLnx Exam Prep is your link from the texbook and lecture to your exams.
The MznLnx Exam Preps are unauthorized and comprehensive reviews of your textbooks.

MznLnx

Rico
Publications

Exam Prep for Management
9th Edition
Robbins & Coulter

Publisher: Raymond Houge
Assistant Editor: Michael Rouger
Text and Cover Designer: Lisa Buckner
Marketing Manager: Sara Swagger
Project Manager, Editorial Production: Jerry Emerson
Art Director: Vernon Lowerui

Product Manager: Dave Mason
Editorial Assitant: Rachel Guzmanji
Pedagogy: Debra Long
Cover Image: Jim Reed/Getty Images
Text and Cover Printer: City Printing, Inc.
Compositor: Media Mix, Inc.

Printed in the United States
ISBN:

For more information about our products, contact us at:
Dave.Mason@RicoPublications.com

For permission to use material from this text or product, submit a request online to:
Dave.Mason@RicoPublications.com

Contents

TO THE STUDENT

COMPREHENSIVE

The *MznLnx* Exam Prep series is designed to help you pass your exams. Editors at MznLnx review your textbooks and then prepare these practice exams to help you master the textbook material. Unlike study guides, workbooks, and practice tests provided by the texbook publisher and textbook authors, *MznLnx* gives you ***all*** of the material in each chapter in exam form, not just samples, so you can be sure to nail your exam.

MECHANICAL

The MznLnx Exam Prep series creates exams that will help you learn the subject matter as well as test you on your understanding. Each question is designed to help you master the concept. Just working through the exams, you gain an understanding of the subject--its a simple mechanical process that produces success.

INTEGRATED STUDY GUIDE AND REVIEW

MznLnx is not just a set of exams designed to test you, its also a comprehensive review of the subject content. Each exam question is also a review of the concept, making sure that you will get the answer correct without having to go to other sources of material. You learn as you go! Its the easiest way to pass an exam.

HUMOR

Studying can be tedious and dry. MznLnx's instructional design includes moderate humor within the exam questions on occassion, to break the tedium and revitalize the brain

1. _________ is a business management strategy, initially implemented by Motorola, that today enjoys widespread application in many sectors of industry.

_________ seeks to improve the quality of process outputs by identifying and removing the causes of defects (errors) and variation in manufacturing and business processes. It uses a set of quality management methods, including statistical methods, and creates a special infrastructure of people within the organization ('Black Belts' etc.)

a. Takt time
b. Theory of constraints
c. Production line
d. Six Sigma

2. _________ is a civil designation for persons who are incorporated in a fixed or permanent way to a society or group: regular member of the working staff, permanent staff distinguished from a supernumerary.

The term '_________' and its counterpart, 'supernumerary,' originated in Spanish and Latin American academy and government; it is now also used in countries all over the world, such as France, the U.S., England, Italy, etc.

There are _________ members of surgical organizations, of universities, of gastronomical associations, etc.

a. Affiliation
b. Adam Smith
c. Abraham Harold Maslow
d. Numerary

3. The _________ captures an expanded spectrum of values and criteria for measuring organizational success: economic, ecological and social. With the ratification of the United Nations and ICLEI _________ standard for urban and community accounting in early 2007, this became the dominant approach to public sector full cost accounting. Similar UN standards apply to natural capital and human capital measurement to assist in measurements required by _________, e.g. the ecoBudget standard for reporting ecological footprint.

a. 33 Strategies of War
b. 28-hour day
c. Triple bottom line
d. 1990 Clean Air Act

4. A _________ is a list of the general tasks and responsibilities of a position. Typically, it also includes to whom the position reports, specifications such as the qualifications needed by the person in the job, salary range for the position, etc. A _________ is usually developed by conducting a job analysis, which includes examining the tasks and sequences of tasks necessary to perform the job.

a. Job description
b. Recruitment advertising
c. Recruitment Process Insourcing
d. Recruitment

5. _________ consists of the mental process of thinking involved with the process of judging the merits of multiple options and selecting one of them for action. Some simple examples include deciding whether to get up in the morning or go back to sleep, or selecting a given route for a journey. More complex examples (often decisions that affect what a person thinks or their core beliefs) include choosing a lifestyle, religious affiliation, or political position.

a. Groups decision making
b. Championship mobilization
c. Trade study
d. Choice

6. '_________' refers to mental and communicative algorithms applied during social communications and interactions in order to reach certain effects or results. The term '_________' is used often in business contexts to refer to the measure of a person's ability to operate within business organizations through social communication and interactions. _________ are how people relate to one another.

a. A Stake in the Outcome
b. A4e
c. AAAI
d. Interpersonal skills

7. _________ is an advertisement in which a particular product specifically mentions a competitor by name for the express purpose of showing why the competitor is inferior to the product naming it.

This should not be confused with parody advertisements, where a fictional product is being advertised for the purpose of poking fun at the particular advertisement, nor should it be confused with the use of a coined brand name for the purpose of comparing the product without actually naming an actual competitor. ('Wikipedia tastes better and is less filling than the Encyclopedia Galactica.')

In the 1980s, during what has been referred to as the cola wars, soft-drink manufacturer Pepsi ran a series of advertisements where people, caught on hidden camera, in a blind taste test, chose Pepsi over rival Coca-Cola.

a. 33 Strategies of War
b. 1990 Clean Air Act
c. 28-hour day
d. Comparative advertising

8. _________ is the provision of service to customers before, during and after a purchase.

According to Turban et al. (2002), '_________ is a series of activities designed to enhance the level of customer satisfaction - that is, the feeling that a product or service has met the customer expectation.'

Its importance varies by product, industry and customer; defective or broken merchandise can be exchanged, often only with a receipt and within a specified time frame.

a. Customer service
b. 28-hour day
c. Service rate
d. 1990 Clean Air Act

9. _________ is a term defined by the Oxford English Dictionary as an individual's 'course or progress through life '. It is usually considered to pertain to remunerative work (and sometimes also formal education.)

The etymology of the term is somewhat ironic in that it comes from the Latin word carrera, which means race .

a. Nursing shortage
b. Spatial mismatch
c. Career planning
d. Career

1. The _________ was a period in the late 18th and early 19th centuries when major changes in agriculture, manufacturing, mining, and transportation had a profound effect on the socioeconomic and cultural conditions in Britain. The changes subsequently spread throughout Europe, North America, and eventually the world. The onset of the _________ marked a major turning point in human society; almost every aspect of daily life was eventually influenced in some way.

a. Adam Smith
b. Affiliation
c. Abraham Harold Maslow
d. Industrial Revolution

2. The _________ is a monograph published by Frederick Winslow Taylor in 1911. This influential monograph is the basis of modern organization and decision theory and has motivated administrators and students of managerial technique. Taylor was an American mechanical engineer and a management consultant in his later years.

a. 33 Strategies of War
b. 1990 Clean Air Act
c. Principles of Scientific Management
d. 28-hour day

3. _________ is a theory of management that analyzes and synthesizes workflows, with the objective of improving labour productivity. The core ideas of the theory were developed by Frederick Winslow Taylor in the 1880s and 1890s, and were first published in his monographs, Shop Management and The Principles of _________ Taylor believed that decisions based upon tradition and rules of thumb should be replaced by precise procedures developed after careful study of an individual at work.

a. Value engineering
b. Capacity planning
c. Master production schedule
d. Scientific Management

4. _________ refers to bodies of techniques for investigating phenomena, acquiring new knowledge, or correcting and integrating previous knowledge. To be termed scientific, a method of inquiry must be based on gathering observable, empirical and measurable evidence subject to specific principles of reasoning. A _________ consists of the collection of data through observation and experimentation, and the formulation and testing of hypotheses.

a. 33 Strategies of War
b. 28-hour day
c. Scientific method
d. 1990 Clean Air Act

5. _________ can be regarded as an outcome of mental processes (cognitive process) leading to the selection of a course of action among several alternatives. Every _________ process produces a final choice. The output can be an action or an opinion of choice.

a. 33 Strategies of War
b. 28-hour day
c. 1990 Clean Air Act
d. Decision making

6. The _________ captures an expanded spectrum of values and criteria for measuring organizational success: economic, ecological and social. With the ratification of the United Nations and ICLEI _________ standard for urban and community accounting in early 2007, this became the dominant approach to public sector full cost accounting. Similar UN standards apply to natural capital and human capital measurement to assist in measurements required by _________, e.g. the ecoBudget standard for reporting ecological footprint.
a. Triple bottom line
b. 1990 Clean Air Act
c. 33 Strategies of War
d. 28-hour day

7. _________ is an economic and social system in which trade and industry are privately controlled for profit. The means of production, which is otherwise known as capital and includes land are owned, operated, and traded for the purpose of generating profits, without force or fraud, by private individuals either singly or jointly. Investments, distribution, income, production, pricing and supply of goods, commodities and services are determined by voluntary private decision in _________, which is also known as a market economy.
a. Adam Smith
b. Abraham Harold Maslow
c. Affiliation
d. Capitalism

8. _________ in its literal sense is the process of transformation of local or regional phenomena into global ones. It can be described as a process by which the people of the world are unified into a single society and function together.

This process is a combination of economic, technological, sociocultural and political forces.

a. Cost Management
b. Histogram
c. Collaborative Planning, Forecasting and Replenishment
d. Globalization

9. The term '_________' refers to the concept of collecting information and attempting to spot a pattern in the information. In some fields of study, the term '_________' has more formally-defined meanings.

In project management _________ is a mathematical technique that uses historical results to predict future outcome.

a. Regression analysis
b. Least squares
c. Stepwise regression
d. Trend analysis

10. _________ is subcontracting a process, such as product design or manufacturing, to a third-party company. The decision to outsource is often made in the interest of lowering cost or making better use of time and energy costs, redirecting or conserving energy directed at the competencies of a particular business, or to make more efficient use of land, labor, capital, (information) technology and resources. _________ became part of the business lexicon during the 1980s.

a. Operant conditioning
b. Opinion leadership
c. Unemployment insurance
d. Outsourcing

11. _________ is a term used to describe the demographic cohort following Generation X. Its members are often referred to as 'Millennials' or 'Echo Boomers') . There are no precise dates for when Gen Y begins and ends. Most commentators use dates from the early 1980s to early 1990s.

a. Giovanni Agnelli
b. Benjamin R. Barber
c. David Wittig
d. Generation Y

12. The _________ is the labour pool in employment. It is generally used to describe those working for a single company or industry, but can also apply to a geographic region like a city, country, state, etc. The term generally excludes the employers or management, and implies those involved in manual labour.

a. Workforce
b. Division of labour
c. Work-life balance
d. Pink-collar worker

13. The 'business case for _________', theorizes that in a global marketplace, a company that employs a diverse workforce (both men and women, people of many generations, people from ethnically and racially diverse backgrounds etc.) is better able to understand the demographics of the marketplace it serves and is thus better equipped to thrive in that marketplace than a company that has a more limited range of employee demographics.

An additional corollary suggests that a company that supports the _________ of its workforce can also improve employee satisfaction, productivity and retention.

a. Virtual team
b. Kanban
c. Diversity
d. Trademark

14. _________ according to Onuoha (2007) is the practice of starting new organizations or revitalizing mature organizations, particularly new businesses generally in response to identified opportunities. _________ is often a difficult undertaking, as a vast majority of new businesses fail. Entrepreneurial activities are substantially different depending on the type of organization that is being started.

a. A Stake in the Outcome
b. A4e
c. AAAI
d. Entrepreneurship

15. An _________ is a person who has possession of an enterprise and assumes significant accountability for the inherent risks and the outcome. It is an ambitious leader who combines land, labor, and capital to create and market new goods or services. The term is a loanword from French and was first defined by the Irish economist Richard Cantillon.

a. A Stake in the Outcome
b. A4e
c. AAAI
d. Entrepreneur

16. _________, commonly referred to as 'eBusiness' or 'e-Business', may be defined as the utilization of information and communication technologies (ICT) in support of all the activities of business. Commerce constitutes the exchange of products and services between businesses, groups and individuals and hence can be seen as one of the essential activities of any business. Hence, electronic commerce or eCommerce focuses on the use of ICT to enable the external activities and relationships of the business with individuals, groups and other businesses .

a. A4e
b. A Stake in the Outcome
c. AAAI
d. Electronic business

17. _________, commonly known as e-commerce, consists of the buying and selling of products or services over electronic systems such as the Internet and other computer networks. The amount of trade conducted electronically has grown extraordinarily with widespread Internet usage. The use of commerce is conducted in this way, spurring and drawing on innovations in electronic funds transfer, supply chain management, Internet marketing, online transaction processing, electronic data interchange (EDI), inventory management systems, and automated data collection systems.

a. Electronic Commerce
b. A Stake in the Outcome
c. A4e
d. Online shopping

18. An _________ is a private computer network that uses Internet technologies to securely share any part of an organization's information or operational systems with its employees. Sometimes the term refers only to the organization's internal website, but often it is a more extensive part of the organization's computer infrastructure and private websites are an important component and focal point of internal communication and collaboration.

An _________ is built from the same concepts and technologies used for the Internet, such as client-server computing and the Internet Protocol Suite (TCP/IP.)

a. A Stake in the Outcome
b. AAAI
c. A4e
d. Intranet

19. _________ comprises a range of practices used in an organisation to identify, create, represent, distribute and enable adoption of insights and experiences. Such insights and experiences comprise knowledge, either embodied in individuals or embedded in organisational processes or practice.

An established discipline since 1991 , _________ includes courses taught in the fields of business administration, information systems, management, and library and information sciences .

a. 33 Strategies of War
b. Knowledge management
c. 28-hour day
d. 1990 Clean Air Act

20. A _________ is the term given to a company that facilitates the learning of its members and continuously transforms itself. _________s develop as a result of the pressures facing modern organizations and enables them to remain competitive in the business environment. A _________ has five main features; systems thinking, personal mastery, mental models, shared vision and team learning.

a. 1990 Clean Air Act
b. Hoshin Kanri
c. Quality function deployment
d. Learning organization

21. _________ is an integrated communications-based process through which individuals and communities discover that existing and newly-identified needs and wants may be satisfied by the products and services of others.

_________ is defined by the American _________ Association as the activity, set of institutions, and processes for creating, communicating, delivering, and exchanging offerings that have value for customers, clients, partners, and society at large. The term developed from the original meaning which referred literally to going to market, as in shopping, or going to a market to buy or sell goods or services.

a. Disruptive technology
b. Customer relationship management
c. Market development
d. Marketing

22. _________ is a civil designation for persons who are incorporated in a fixed or permanent way to a society or group: regular member of the working staff, permanent staff distinguished from a supernumerary.

The term '_________' and its counterpart, 'supernumerary,' originated in Spanish and Latin American academy and government; it is now also used in countries all over the world, such as France, the U.S., England, Italy, etc.

There are _________ members of surgical organizations, of universities, of gastronomical associations, etc.

a. Numerary
b. Affiliation
c. Abraham Harold Maslow
d. Adam Smith

23. _________ can be considered to have three main components: quality control, quality assurance and quality improvement. _________ is focused not only on product quality, but also the means to achieve it. _________ therefore uses quality assurance and control of processes as well as products to achieve more consistent quality.
a. 1990 Clean Air Act
b. Total quality management
c. 28-hour day
d. Quality management

24. _________ is a business management strategy aimed at embedding awareness of quality in all organizational processes. _________ has been widely used in manufacturing, education, hospitals, call centers, government, and service industries, as well as NASA space and science programs.

As defined by the International Organization for Standardization (ISO):

> '_________ is a management approach for an organization, centered on quality, based on the participation of all its members and aiming at long-term success through customer satisfaction, and benefits to all members of the organization and to society.' ISO 8402:1994

One major aim is to reduce variation from every process so that greater consistency of effort is obtained. (Royse, D., Thyer, B., Padgett D., ' Logan T., 2006)

a. Quality management
b. Total quality management
c. 1990 Clean Air Act
d. 28-hour day

25. _________ is a process or productivity improvement tool intended to have a stable and consistent growth and improvement of all the segments of a process or processes. _________ ensures the process stabilization and further improvement. When an organization's growth and development is intended, identification of all the processes and development of a measurement analysis of each process step is necessary.

a. 1990 Clean Air Act
b. Continual improvement
c. 33 Strategies of War
d. 28-hour day

1. _________ is one of the managerial functions like planning, organizing, staffing and directing. It is an important function because it helps to check the errors and to take the corrective action so that deviation from standards are minimized and stated goals of the organization are achieved in desired manner.According to modern concepts, _________ is a foreseeing action whereas earlier concept of _________ was used only when errors were detected. _________ in management means setting standards, measuring actual performance and taking corrective action.

a. Schedule of reinforcement
b. Decision tree pruning
c. Turnover
d. Control

2. _________ is an idea in the field of Organizational studies and management which describes the psychology, attitudes, experiences, beliefs and Values (personal and cultural values) of an organization. It has been defined as 'the specific collection of values and norms that are shared by people and groups in an organization and that control the way they interact with each other and with stakeholders outside the organization.'

This definition continues to explain organizational values also known as 'beliefs and ideas about what kinds of goals members of an organization should pursue and ideas about the appropriate kinds or standards of behavior organizational members should use to achieve these goals. From organizational values develop organizational norms, guidelines or expectations that prescribe appropriate kinds of behavior by employees in particular situations and control the behavior of organizational members towards one another.'

_________ is not the same as corporate culture.

a. Organizational effectiveness
b. Organizational culture
c. Union shop
d. Organizational development

3. _________ is a civil designation for persons who are incorporated in a fixed or permanent way to a society or group: regular member of the working staff, permanent staff distinguished from a supernumerary.

The term '_________' and its counterpart, 'supernumerary,' originated in Spanish and Latin American academy and government; it is now also used in countries all over the world, such as France, the U.S., England, Italy, etc.

There are _________ members of surgical organizations, of universities, of gastronomical associations, etc.

a. Affiliation
b. Numerary
c. Abraham Harold Maslow
d. Adam Smith

4. The _________ captures an expanded spectrum of values and criteria for measuring organizational success: economic, ecological and social. With the ratification of the United Nations and ICLEI _________ standard for urban and community accounting in early 2007, this became the dominant approach to public sector full cost accounting. Similar UN standards apply to natural capital and human capital measurement to assist in measurements required by _________, e.g. the ecoBudget standard for reporting ecological footprint.

a. Triple bottom line
b. 28-hour day
c. 1990 Clean Air Act
d. 33 Strategies of War

5. In game theory, an _________ is a set of moves or strategies taken by the players, or their payoffs resulting from the actions or strategies taken by all players. The two are complementary in that given knowledge of the set of strategies of all players, the final state of the game is known, as are any relevant payoffs. In a game where chance or a random event is involved, the _________ is not known from only the set of strategies, but is only realized when the random event(s) are realized.

a. Outcome
b. A Stake in the Outcome
c. A4e
d. AAAI

6. The 'business case for _________', theorizes that in a global marketplace, a company that employs a diverse workforce (both men and women, people of many generations, people from ethnically and racially diverse backgrounds etc.) is better able to understand the demographics of the marketplace it serves and is thus better equipped to thrive in that marketplace than a company that has a more limited range of employee demographics.

An additional corollary suggests that a company that supports the _________ of its workforce can also improve employee satisfaction, productivity and retention.

a. Virtual team
b. Diversity
c. Trademark
d. Kanban

7. The _________ is the labour pool in employment. It is generally used to describe those working for a single company or industry, but can also apply to a geographic region like a city, country, state, etc. The term generally excludes the employers or management, and implies those involved in manual labour.

a. Work-life balance
b. Pink-collar worker
c. Division of labour
d. Workforce

8. _________ refers to increasing the spiritual, political, social or economic strength of individuals and communities. It often involves the empowered developing confidence in their own capacities.

The term Human _________ covers a vast landscape of meanings, interpretations, definitions and disciplines ranging from psychology and philosophy to the highly commercialized Self-Help industry and Motivational sciences.

a. Empowerment
b. AAAI
c. A Stake in the Outcome
d. A4e

9. A mutual shareholder or _________ is an individual or company (including a corporation) that legally owns one or more shares of stock in a joint stock company. A company's shareholders collectively own that company. Thus, the typical goal of such companies is to enhance shareholder value.
a. Free riding
b. 1990 Clean Air Act
c. Stockholder
d. Shareholder

10. The _________ of 1990 (ADA) is the short title of United States (Pub.L. 101-336, 104 Stat. 327, enacted July 26, 1990), codified at 42 U.S.C. Â§ 12101 et seq. It was signed into law on July 26, 1990, by President George H. W. Bush, and later amended with changes effective January 1, 2009. The ADA is a wide-ranging civil rights law that prohibits, under certain circumstances, discrimination based on disability. It affords similar protections against discrimination to Americans with disabilities as the Civil Rights Act of 1964,
a. Australian labour law
b. Equal Pay Act of 1963
c. Employment discrimination
d. Americans with Disabilities Act

11. _________ or _________ data refers to selected population characteristics as used in government, marketing or opinion research, or the _________ profiles used in such research. Note the distinction from the term 'demography' Commonly-used _________s include race, age, income, disabilities, mobility (in terms of travel time to work or number of vehicles available), educational attainment, home ownership, employment status, and even location.

a. Abraham Harold Maslow
b. Adam Smith
c. Affiliation
d. Demographic

12. _________, commonly abbreviated to Gen X, is a term used to refer to a generational cohort of children born after the baby boom ended and usually prior to the 1980s

The term _________ has been used in demography, the social sciences, and marketing, though it is most often used in popular culture.

In the U.S. _________ was originally referred to as the 'baby bust' generation because of the drop in the birth rate following the baby boom.

a. Generation X
b. Adam Smith
c. Affiliation
d. Abraham Harold Maslow

13. _________ is a term used to describe the demographic cohort following Generation X. Its members are often referred to as 'Millennials' or 'Echo Boomers') . There are no precise dates for when Gen Y begins and ends. Most commentators use dates from the early 1980s to early 1990s.

a. David Wittig
b. Giovanni Agnelli
c. Benjamin R. Barber
d. Generation Y

14. _________ is the concept of how effective an organization is in achieving the outcomes the organization intends to produce. The idea of _________ is especially important for non-profit organizations as most people who donate money to non-profit organizations and charities are interested in knowing whether the organization is effective in accomplishing its goals.

An organization's effectiveness is also dependent on its communicative competence and ethics.

a. Organizational effectiveness
b. Organizational structure
c. Organizational development
d. Informal organization

1. The _________ is an international organization designed by its founders to supervise and liberalize international trade. The organization officially commenced on 1 January 1995, under the Marrakesh Agreement, succeeding the 1947 General Agreement on Tariffs and Trade (GATT.)

The _________ deals with regulation of trade between participating countries; it provides a framework for negotiating and formalising trade agreements, and a dispute resolution process aimed at enforcing participants' adherence to _________ agreements which are signed by representatives of member governments and ratified by their parliaments.

a. 1990 Clean Air Act
b. Network planning and design
c. National Institute for Occupational Safety and Health
d. World Trade Organization

2. _________ is subcontracting a process, such as product design or manufacturing, to a third-party company. The decision to outsource is often made in the interest of lowering cost or making better use of time and energy costs, redirecting or conserving energy directed at the competencies of a particular business, or to make more efficient use of land, labor, capital, (information) technology and resources. _________ became part of the business lexicon during the 1980s.

a. Unemployment insurance
b. Outsourcing
c. Opinion leadership
d. Operant conditioning

3. The _________ captures an expanded spectrum of values and criteria for measuring organizational success: economic, ecological and social. With the ratification of the United Nations and ICLEI _________ standard for urban and community accounting in early 2007, this became the dominant approach to public sector full cost accounting. Similar UN standards apply to natural capital and human capital measurement to assist in measurements required by _________, e.g. the ecoBudget standard for reporting ecological footprint.

a. Triple bottom line
b. 28-hour day
c. 33 Strategies of War
d. 1990 Clean Air Act

4. _________ is a type of trade policy that allows traders to act and transact without interference from government. Thus, the policy permits trading partners mutual gains from trade, with goods and services produced according to the theory of comparative advantage.

Under a _________ policy, prices are a reflection of true supply and demand, and are the sole determinant of resource allocation.

a. 28-hour day
b. 1990 Clean Air Act
c. 33 Strategies of War
d. Free Trade

5. _________ is a designated group of countries that have agreed to eliminate tariffs, quotas and preferences on most (if not all) goods and services traded between them. It can be considered the second stage of economic integration. Countries choose this kind of economic integration form if their economical structures are complementary.
a. 28-hour day
b. Free trade area
c. 33 Strategies of War
d. 1990 Clean Air Act

6. The _________ is a trilateral trade bloc in North America created by the governments of the United States, Canada, and Mexico. The agreement creating the trade bloc came into force on January 1, 1994. It superseded the Canada-United States Free Trade Agreement between the U.S. and Canada.
a. North American Free Trade Agreement
b. Trade union
c. Business war game
d. Career portfolios

7. _________ refers to the methods of practicing and using another person's business philosophy. The franchisor grants the independent operator the right to distribute its products, techniques, and trademarks for a percentage of gross monthly sales and a royalty fee. Various tangibles and intangibles such as national or international advertising, training, and other support services are commonly made available by the franchisor.
a. Franchising
b. ServiceMaster
c. 28-hour day
d. 1990 Clean Air Act

8. The _________ was the outcome of the failure of negotiating governments to create the International Trade Organization (ITO.) GATT was formed in 1947 and lasted until 1994, when it was replaced by the World Trade Organization. The Bretton Woods Conference had introduced the idea for an organization to regulate trade as part of a larger plan for economic recovery after World War II.

a. Multilateral treaty
b. 28-hour day
c. 1990 Clean Air Act
d. General Agreement on Tariffs and Trade

9. A _________ or transnational corporation is a corporation or enterprise that manages production or delivers services in more than one country. It can also be referred to as an international corporation.

The first modern _________ is generally thought to be the Dutch East India Company, established in 1602.

a. Small and medium enterprises
b. Financial Accounting Standards Board
c. Command center
d. Multinational corporation

10. An _________ is a person who has possession of an enterprise and assumes significant accountability for the inherent risks and the outcome. It is an ambitious leader who combines land, labor, and capital to create and market new goods or services. The term is a loanword from French and was first defined by the Irish economist Richard Cantillon.
a. A4e
b. Entrepreneur
c. AAAI
d. A Stake in the Outcome

11. _________ is a term used to describe practice of sourcing from the global market for goods and services across geopolitical boundaries. _________ often aims to exploit global efficiencies in the delivery of a product or service. These efficiencies include low cost skilled labor, low cost raw material and other economic factors like tax breaks and low trade tariffs.
a. Purchase requisition
b. Purchasing process
c. 1990 Clean Air Act
d. Global sourcing

12. In business, the term word _________ refers to a number of procurement practices, aimed at finding, evaluating and engaging suppliers of goods and services:

- Global _________, a procurement strategy aimed at exploiting global efficiencies in production
- Strategic _________, a component of supply chain management, for improving and re-evaluating purchasing activities
- _________, the identification of job candidates through proactive recruiting technique
- Co-_________, a type of auditing service
- Low-cost country _________, a procurement strategy for acquiring materials from countries with lower labour and production costs in order to cut operating expenses
- Corporate _________, a supply chain, purchasing/procurement, and inventory function
- Second-tier _________, a practice of rewarding suppliers for attempting to achieve minority-owned business spending goals of their customer
- Netsourcing, a practice of utilizing an established group of businesses, individuals, or hardware ' software applications to streamline or initiate procurement practices by tapping in to and working through a third party provider
- Inverted _________, a price volatility reduction strategy usually conducted by procurement or supply-chain person by which the value of an organization's waste-stream is maximized by actively seeking out the highest price possible from a range of potential buyers exploiting price trends and other market factors
- Multisourcing, a strategy that treats a given function, such as IT, as a portfolio of activities, some of which should be outsourced and others of which should be performed by internal staff.
- Crowdsourcing, using an undefined, generally large group of people or community in the form of an open call to perform a task

In journalism, it can also refer to:

- Journalism _________, the practice of identifying a person or publication that gives information
- Single _________, the reuse of content in publishing

In computing, it can refer to:

- Open-_________, the act of releasing previously proprietary software under an open source/free software license
- Power _________ equipment, network devices that will provide power in a Power over Ethernet (PoE) setup

.

a. Cost Management
b. Continuous
c. Sourcing
d. Reinforcement

13. _________ is exchange of capital, goods, and services across international borders or territories. In most countries, it represents a significant share of gross domestic product (GDP.) While _________ has been present throughout much of history , its economic, social, and political importance has been on the rise in recent centuries.

a. A4e
b. AAAI
c. International trade
d. A Stake in the Outcome

14. A _________ is an entity formed between two or more parties to undertake economic activity together. The parties agree to create a new entity by both contributing equity, and they then share in the revenues, expenses, and control of the enterprise. The venture can be for one specific project only, or a continuing business relationship such as the Fuji Xerox _________.

a. Patent
b. Meritor Savings Bank v. Vinson
c. Civil Rights Act of 1991
d. Joint venture

15. A _________ is a type of business entity in which partners (owners) share with each other the profits or losses of the business. _________s are often favored over corporations for taxation purposes, as the _________ structure does not generally incur a tax on profits before it is distributed to the partners (i.e. there is no dividend tax levied.) However, depending on the _________ structure and the jurisdiction in which it operates, owners of a _________ may be exposed to greater personal liability than they would as shareholders of a corporation.

a. Federal Employers Liability Act
b. Mediation
c. Due process
d. Partnership

16. A _________ is a formal relationship between two or more parties to pursue a set of agreed upon goals or to meet a critical business need while remaining independent organizations.

Partners may provide the _________ with resources such as products, distribution channels, manufacturing capability, project funding, capital equipment, knowledge, expertise, or intellectual property. The alliance is a cooperation or collaboration which aims for a synergy where each partner hopes that the benefits from the alliance will be greater than those from individual efforts.

a. Farmshoring
b. Golden parachute
c. Process automation
d. Strategic alliance

17. _________ is a mathematical science pertaining to the collection, analysis, interpretation or explanation, and presentation of data. It also provides tools for prediction and forecasting based on data. It is applicable to a wide variety of academic disciplines, from the natural and social sciences to the humanities, government and business.

a. Location parameter
b. Simple moving average
c. Failure rate
d. Statistics

18. A _________, in business matters, is an entity that is controlled by a bigger and more powerful entity. The controlled entity is called a company, corporation, or limited liability company and in some cases can be a government or state-owned enterprise, and the controlling entity is called its parent (or the parent company.) The reason for this distinction is that a lone company cannot be a _________ of any organization; only an entity representing a legal fiction as a separate entity can be a _________.

a. Subsidiary
b. 33 Strategies of War
c. 1990 Clean Air Act
d. 28-hour day

19. In economics, business, retail, and accounting, a _________ is the value of money that has been used up to produce something, and hence is not available for use anymore. In economics, a _________ is an alternative that is given up as a result of a decision. In business, the _________ may be one of acquisition, in which case the amount of money expended to acquire it is counted as _________.

a. Cost overrun
b. Fixed costs
c. Cost allocation
d. Cost

20. In finance, the _________s between two currencies specifies how much one currency is worth in terms of the other. It is the value of a foreign nation's currency in terms of the home nation's currency. For example an _________ of 102 Japanese yen to the United States dollar means that JPY 102 is worth the same as USD 1.

a. Exchange rate
b. A Stake in the Outcome
c. AAAI
d. A4e

21. In economics, _________ is a rise in the general level of prices of goods and services in an economy over a period of time. When the general price level rises, each unit of the functional currency buys fewer goods and services; consequently, _________ is a decline in the real value of money--a loss of purchasing power in the internal medium of exchange which is also the monetary unit of account in an economy. A chief measure of general price-level _________ is the general _________ rate, which is the percentage change in a general price index (normally the Consumer Price Index) over time.

a. A4e
b. Economy
c. A Stake in the Outcome
d. Inflation

22. A chief executive officer (_________) or chief executive is one of the highest-ranking corporate officer (executive) or administrator in charge of total management. An individual selected as President and _________ of a corporation, company, organization, or agency, reports to the board of directors. In internal communication and press releases, many companies capitalize the term and those of other high positions, even when they are not proper nouns.

a. Director of communications
b. Portfolio manager
c. CEO
d. Chief executive officer

23. _________ has been described as the 'process of social influence in which one person can enlist the aid and support of others in the accomplishment of a common task' . A definition more inclusive of followers comes from Alan Keith of Genentech who said '_________ is ultimately about creating a way for people to contribute to making something extraordinary happen.'

_________ is one of the most salient aspects of the organizational context. However, defining _________ has been challenging.

a. 28-hour day
b. 1990 Clean Air Act
c. Situational leadership
d. Leadership

24. _________ is a term used to describe any moral, political that stresses human interdependence and the importance of a collective, rather than the importance of separate individuals. Collectivists focus on community and society, and seek to give priority to group goals over individual goals. The philosophical underpinnings of _________ are for some related to holism or organicism - the view that the whole is greater than the sum of its parts/pieces.

a. 28-hour day
b. 1990 Clean Air Act
c. Collaborative methods
d. Collectivism

1. A mutual shareholder or _________ is an individual or company (including a corporation) that legally owns one or more shares of stock in a joint stock company. A company's shareholders collectively own that company. Thus, the typical goal of such companies is to enhance shareholder value.

a. Free riding
b. 1990 Clean Air Act
c. Stockholder
d. Shareholder

2. A _________ is a process in which a potential employee is evaluated by an employer for prospective employment in their company, organization and was established in the late 16th century.

A _________ typically precedes the hiring decision, and is used to evaluate the candidate. The interview is usually preceded by the evaluation of submitted résumés from interested candidates, then selecting a small number of candidates for interviews.

a. Payrolling
b. Split shift
c. Supported employment
d. Job interview

3. The term '_________' refers to the concept of collecting information and attempting to spot a pattern in the information. In some fields of study, the term '_________' has more formally-defined meanings.

In project management _________ is a mathematical technique that uses historical results to predict future outcome.

a. Stepwise regression
b. Regression analysis
c. Least squares
d. Trend analysis

4. _________ refers to the overarching strategy of the diversified firm. Such a _________ answers the questions of 'in which businesses should we be in?' and 'how does being in these business create synergy and/or add to the competitive advantage of the corporation as a whole?'

Business strategy refers to the aggregated strategies of single business firm or a strategic business unit (SBU) in a diversified corporation. According to Michael Porter, a firm must formulate a business strategy that incorporates either cost leadership, differentiation or focus in order to achieve a sustainable competitive advantage and long-term success in its chosen arenas or industries.

a. Strategic group
b. Competitive heterogeneity
c. Strategic drift
d. Corporate strategy

5. _________ is a term in psychology which refers to a person's belief about what causes the good or bad results in his or her life, either in general or in a specific area such as health or academics. Understanding of the concept was developed by Julian B. Rotter in 1954, and has since become an important aspect of personality studies.

_________ refers to the extent to which individuals believe that they can control events that affect them.

a. Locus of control
b. Self-enhancement
c. Machiavellianism
d. Social loafing

6. _________ is one of the managerial functions like planning, organizing, staffing and directing. It is an important function because it helps to check the errors and to take the corrective action so that deviation from standards are minimized and stated goals of the organization are achieved in desired manner.According to modern concepts, _________ is a foreseeing action whereas earlier concept of _________ was used only when errors were detected. _________ in management means setting standards, measuring actual performance and taking corrective action.

a. Schedule of reinforcement
b. Decision tree pruning
c. Turnover
d. Control

7. The _________ captures an expanded spectrum of values and criteria for measuring organizational success: economic, ecological and social. With the ratification of the United Nations and ICLEI _________ standard for urban and community accounting in early 2007, this became the dominant approach to public sector full cost accounting. Similar UN standards apply to natural capital and human capital measurement to assist in measurements required by _________, e.g. the ecoBudget standard for reporting ecological footprint.

a. 28-hour day
b. 33 Strategies of War
c. 1990 Clean Air Act
d. Triple bottom line

8. The _________ of 1977 (15 U.S.C. Â§Â§ 78dd-1, et seq.) is a United States federal law known primarily for two of its main provisions, one that addresses accounting transparency requirements under the Securities Exchange Act of 1934 and another concerning bribery of foreign officials.

a. Foreign Corrupt Practices Act
b. Meritor Savings Bank v. Vinson
c. Limited liability
d. Social Security Act of 1965

9. The United Nations _________ is an United Nations initiative to encourage businesses worldwide to adopt sustainable and socially responsible policies, and to report on their implementation. The _________ is a principle based framework for businesses, stating ten principles in the areas of human rights, labour, the environment and anti-corruption. Under the _________, companies are brought together with UN agencies, labour groups and civil society.

a. Global Compact
b. 28-hour day
c. 33 Strategies of War
d. 1990 Clean Air Act

10. A chief executive officer (_________) or chief executive is one of the highest-ranking corporate officer (executive) or administrator in charge of total management. An individual selected as President and _________ of a corporation, company, organization, or agency, reports to the board of directors. In internal communication and press releases, many companies capitalize the term and those of other high positions, even when they are not proper nouns.

a. Portfolio manager
b. Director of communications
c. Chief executive officer
d. CEO

11. A set of _________ is the verbal equivalent of a graphical decision tree, which specifies class membership based on a hierarchical sequence of (contingent) decisions. Each rule in a set of _________ therefore generally takes the form of a Horn clause wherein class membership is implied by a conjunction of contingent observations.

IF condition_1 AND condition_2 AND ...

a. 1990 Clean Air Act
b. Decision rules
c. 33 Strategies of War
d. 28-hour day

12. _________ of the learning curve effect and the closely related experience curve effect express the relationship between equations for experience and efficiency or between efficiency gains and investment in the effort. The experience of 'learning curves' was first observed by the 19th Century German psychologist Hermann Ebbinghaus according to the difficulty of memorizing varying numbers of verbal stimuli, and subsequent learning about the complex processes of learning are discussed in the

.

The rule used for representing the learning curve effect states that the more times a task has been performed, the less time will be required on each subsequent iteration.

a. Point biserial correlation coefficient
b. Distribution
c. Models
d. Spatial Decision Support Systems

13. The _________ of 2002 (Pub.L. 107-204, 116 Stat. 745, enacted July 30, 2002), also known as the Public Company Accounting Reform and Investor Protection Act of 2002 and commonly called Sarbanes-Oxley, Sarbox or SOX, is a United States federal law enacted on July 30, 2002, as a reaction to a number of major corporate and accounting scandals including those affecting Enron, Tyco International, Adelphia, Peregrine Systems and WorldCom.
a. Fair Labor Standards Act
b. Letter of credit
c. Sarbanes-Oxley Act of 2002
d. Sarbanes-Oxley Act

14. _________ has been described as the 'process of social influence in which one person can enlist the aid and support of others in the accomplishment of a common task' . A definition more inclusive of followers comes from Alan Keith of Genentech who said '_________ is ultimately about creating a way for people to contribute to making something extraordinary happen.'

_________ is one of the most salient aspects of the organizational context. However, defining _________ has been challenging.

a. 28-hour day
b. 1990 Clean Air Act
c. Situational leadership
d. Leadership

15. An _________ is a person who has possession of an enterprise and assumes significant accountability for the inherent risks and the outcome. It is an ambitious leader who combines land, labor, and capital to create and market new goods or services. The term is a loanword from French and was first defined by the Irish economist Richard Cantillon.

a. A Stake in the Outcome
b. AAAI
c. A4e
d. Entrepreneur

16. _________ according to Onuoha (2007) is the practice of starting new organizations or revitalizing mature organizations, particularly new businesses generally in response to identified opportunities. _________ is often a difficult undertaking, as a vast majority of new businesses fail. Entrepreneurial activities are substantially different depending on the type of organization that is being started.

a. A4e
b. Entrepreneurship
c. A Stake in the Outcome
d. AAAI

17. An _________ is the negative aspects of human activity on the biophysical environment. Environmentalism, a social and environmental movement that started in the 1960s, focuses on addressing _________s through advocacy, education and activism.

Major current _________s are climate change, pollution and resource depletion.

a. A Stake in the Outcome
b. AAAI
c. A4e
d. Environmental issue

18. The _________ is an international organization designed by its founders to supervise and liberalize international trade. The organization officially commenced on 1 January 1995, under the Marrakesh Agreement, succeeding the 1947 General Agreement on Tariffs and Trade (GATT.)

The _________ deals with regulation of trade between participating countries; it provides a framework for negotiating and formalising trade agreements, and a dispute resolution process aimed at enforcing participants' adherence to _________ agreements which are signed by representatives of member governments and ratified by their parliaments.

a. National Institute for Occupational Safety and Health
b. World Trade Organization
c. Network planning and design
d. 1990 Clean Air Act

1. _________ consists of the mental process of thinking involved with the process of judging the merits of multiple options and selecting one of them for action. Some simple examples include deciding whether to get up in the morning or go back to sleep, or selecting a given route for a journey. More complex examples (often decisions that affect what a person thinks or their core beliefs) include choosing a lifestyle, religious affiliation, or political position.

a. Championship mobilization
b. Groups decision making
c. Trade study
d. Choice

2. A _________ is a list of the general tasks and responsibilities of a position. Typically, it also includes to whom the position reports, specifications such as the qualifications needed by the person in the job, salary range for the position, etc. A _________ is usually developed by conducting a job analysis, which includes examining the tasks and sequences of tasks necessary to perform the job.

a. Recruitment
b. Job description
c. Recruitment advertising
d. Recruitment Process Insourcing

3. _________ can be regarded as an outcome of mental processes (cognitive process) leading to the selection of a course of action among several alternatives. Every _________ process produces a final choice. The output can be an action or an opinion of choice.

a. 1990 Clean Air Act
b. 28-hour day
c. Decision making
d. 33 Strategies of War

4. _________ is a concept based on the fact that rationality of individuals is limited by the information they have, the cognitive limitations of their minds, and the finite amount of time they have to make decisions. This contrasts with the concept of rationality as optimization. Another way to look at _________ is that, because decision-makers lack the ability and resources to arrive at the optimal solution, they instead apply their rationality only after having greatly simplified the choices available.

a. Complete information
b. Mixed strategy
c. Transferable utility
d. Bounded rationality

5. _________ was first described by Barry M. Staw in his 1976 paper, 'Knee deep in the big muddy: A study of escalating commitment to a chosen course of action'. More recently the term Sunk cost fallacy has been used to describe the phenomenon where people justify increased investment in a decision, based on the cumulative prior investment, despite new evidence suggesting that the decision was probably wrong. Such investment may include money , time, or -- in the case of military strategy -- human lives.

a. A Stake in the Outcome
b. Open Options
c. A4e
d. Escalation of commitment

6. A _________ is typically described as a deliberate plan of action to guide decisions and achieve rational outcome(s.) However, the term may also be used to denote what is actually done, even though it is unplanned.

The term may apply to government, private sector organizations and groups, and individuals.

a. 33 Strategies of War
b. 1990 Clean Air Act
c. Policy
d. 28-hour day

7. _________ is a term defined by the Oxford English Dictionary as an individual's 'course or progress through life '. It is usually considered to pertain to remunerative work (and sometimes also formal education.)

The etymology of the term is somewhat ironic in that it comes from the Latin word carrera, which means race .

a. Spatial mismatch
b. Career planning
c. Nursing shortage
d. Career

8. In organizational development (or OD), the study of _________ looks at:

- how individuals manage their careers within and between organizations
- and how organizations structure the career progress of their members, it can also be tied into succession planning within some organizations.

In personal development, _________ is:

- '... the total constellation of psychological, sociological, educational, physical, economic, and chance factors that combine to influence the nature and significance of work in the total lifespan of any given individual.'

- '... the lifelong psychological and behavioral processes as well as contextual influences shaping one's career over the life span. As such, _________ involves the person's creation of a career pattern, decision-making style, integration of life roles, values expression, and life-role self concepts.'

Figures in _________

- Jeff A. Brown
- Jesse B. Davis
- Caela Farren
- John L. Holland
- Kris Magnusson
- Frank Parsons
- Vance Peavy
- Edgar Schein
- Rino Schreuder
- Mark L. Savickas
- Donald Super

.

a. Sole proprietorship
b. Business process reengineering
c. Career development
d. Horizontal integration

9. In probability theory and statistics, the _________ of a random variable is the integral of the random variable with respect to its probability measure. For discrete random variables this is equivalent to the probability-weighted sum of the possible values, and for continuous random variables with a density function it is the probability density -weighted integral of the possible values.

a. AAAI
b. A4e
c. A Stake in the Outcome
d. Expected value

10. In decision theory and estimation theory, the _________ of an estimator, $\hat{\theta}$, of an unknown parameter of the distribution, θ, is the expected value of the loss function

$$R(\theta, \hat{\theta}) = \mathbb{E}_{\theta} L(\theta, \hat{\theta}) = \int L(\theta, \hat{\theta})\, dP_{\theta}.$$

where dP_θ is a probability measure parametrized by θ.

- For a scalar parameter θ and a quadratic loss function,

  $$L(\theta, \hat{\theta}) = (\theta - \hat{\theta})^2$$

  the _________ function becomes the mean squared error of the estimate,

  $$R(\theta, \hat{\theta}) = E_{\theta}(\theta - \hat{\theta})^2$$

- In density estimation, the unknown parameter is probability density itself. The loss function is typically chosen to be a norm in an appropriate function space. For example, for L^2 norm,

  $$L(f, \hat{f}) = \|f - \hat{f}\|_2^2$$

  the _________ function becomes the mean integrated squared error

  $$R(f, \hat{f}) = E\|f - \hat{f}\|^2$$

.

a. Risk aversion
b. Risk
c. Linear model
d. Financial modeling

11. In statistical decision theory, where we are faced with the problem of estimating a deterministic parameter (vector) $\theta \in \Theta$ from observations $x \in \mathcal{X}$, an estimator (estimation rule) δ^M is called _________ if its maximal risk is minimal among all estimators of θ. In a sense this means that δ^M is an estimator which performs best in the worst possible case allowed in the problem.

Consider the problem of estimating a deterministic (not Bayesian) parameter $\theta \in \Theta$ from noisy or corrupt data $x \in \mathcal{X}$ related through the conditional probability distribution $P(x|\theta)$.

a. Minimax
b. Backdating
c. Battle Force Tactical Trainer
d. Control

12. _________ is a way of expressing knowledge or belief that an event will occur or has occurred. In mathematics the concept has been given an exact meaning in _________ theory, that is used extensively in such areas of study as mathematics, statistics, finance, gambling, science, and philosophy to draw conclusions about the likelihood of potential events and the underlying mechanics of complex systems.

The word _________ does not have a consistent direct definition.

a. Statistics
b. Time series analysis
c. Probability
d. Standard deviation

13. _________ is a forward looking process for setting goals and regularly checking progress toward achieving those goals. It is a continual feedback process whereby the actual outputs are measured and compared with the desired goals. Any discrepancy or gap is then fed back into changing the inputs of the process, so as to achieve the desired goals or outputs.
a. Performance management
b. 28-hour day
c. 33 Strategies of War
d. 1990 Clean Air Act

14. _________ refers to the movement of cash into or out of a business or financial product. It is usually measured during a specified, finite period of time. Measurement of _________ can be used

- to determine a project's rate of return or value. The time of _________s into and out of projects are used as inputs in financial models such as internal rate of return, and net present value.
- to determine problems with a business's liquidity. Being profitable does not necessarily mean being liquid. A company can fail because of a shortage of cash, even while profitable.
- as an alternate measure of a business's profits when it is believed that accrual accounting concepts do not represent economic realities. For example, a company may be notionally profitable but generating little operational cash (as may be the case for a company that barters its products rather than selling for cash.) In such a case, the company may be deriving additional operating cash by issuing shares evaluating default risk, re-investment requirements, etc.

_________ is a generic term used differently depending on the context. It may be defined by users for their own purposes.

a. Gross profit
b. Sweat equity
c. Cash flow
d. Gross profit margin

15. Engineering _________ is the permissible limit of variation in

1. a physical dimension,
2. a measured value or physical property of a material, manufactured object, system, or service,
3. other measured values (such as temperature, humidity, etc.)
4. in engineering and safety, a physical distance or space (_________), as in a truck (lorry), train or boat under a bridge as well as a train in a tunnel

Dimensions, properties, or conditions may vary within certain practical limits without significantly affecting functioning of equipment or a process. _________s are specified to allow reasonable leeway for imperfections and inherent variability without compromising performance.

The _________ may be specified as a factor or percentage of the nominal value, a maximum deviation from a nominal value, an explicit range of allowed values, be specified by a note or published standard with this information, or be implied by the numeric accuracy of the nominal value. _________ can be symmetrical, as in 40±0.1, or asymmetrical, such as 40+0.2/−0.1.

a. Tolerance
b. Quality assurance
c. Root cause analysis
d. Zero defects

16. The 'business case for _________', theorizes that in a global marketplace, a company that employs a diverse workforce (both men and women, people of many generations, people from ethnically and racially diverse backgrounds etc.) is better able to understand the demographics of the marketplace it serves and is thus better equipped to thrive in that marketplace than a company that has a more limited range of employee demographics.

An additional corollary suggests that a company that supports the _________ of its workforce can also improve employee satisfaction, productivity and retention.

a. Kanban
b. Virtual team
c. Diversity
d. Trademark

17. The _________ is the labour pool in employment. It is generally used to describe those working for a single company or industry, but can also apply to a geographic region like a city, country, state, etc. The term generally excludes the employers or management, and implies those involved in manual labour.

a. Work-life balance
b. Division of labour
c. Pink-collar worker
d. Workforce

18. _________ is an adjective for experience-based techniques that help in problem solving, learning and discovery. A _________ method is particularly used to rapidly come to a solution that is hoped to be close to the best possible answer, or 'optimal solution'. _________s are 'rules of thumb', educated guesses, intuitive judgments or simply common sense.

a. Heuristic
b. Representativeness
c. 1990 Clean Air Act
d. 28-hour day

19. In psychology and cognitive science, _________ is a tendency to search for or interpret new information in a way that confirms one's preconceptions and to irrationally avoid information and interpretations which contradict prior beliefs. _________ is a type of cognitive bias and represents an error of inductive inference, or as a form of selection bias toward confirmation of the hypothesis under study or disconfirmation of an alternative hypothesis.

_________ is of interest in the teaching of critical thinking, as the skill (of thinking critically) is misused if rigorous critical scrutiny is applied only to evidence challenging a preconceived idea but not to evidence supporting it.

a. Cognitive biases
b. Self-serving bias
c. Choice-supportive bias
d. Confirmation bias

20. A _________ occurs when people attribute their successes to internal or personal factors but attribute their failures to situational factors beyond their control. The _________ can be seen in the common human tendency to take credit for success but to deny responsibility for failure. It may also manifest itself as a tendency for people to evaluate ambiguous information in a way that is beneficial to their interests.

a. Halo effect
b. Self-serving bias
c. Pygmalion effect
d. Fundamental attribution error

21. In economics and business decision-making, _________ are costs that cannot be recovered once they have been incurred. _________ are sometimes contrasted with variable costs, which are the costs that will change due to the proposed course of action, and prospective costs which are costs that will be incurred if an action is taken.

In traditional microeconomic theory, only variable costs are relevant to a decision.

a. Pygmalion effect
b. Cognitive biases
c. Fundamental attribution error
d. Sunk costs

22. In economics, business, retail, and accounting, a _________ is the value of money that has been used up to produce something, and hence is not available for use anymore. In economics, a _________ is an alternative that is given up as a result of a decision. In business, the _________ may be one of acquisition, in which case the amount of money expended to acquire it is counted as _________.

a. Cost overrun
b. Cost
c. Fixed costs
d. Cost allocation

1. The _________ captures an expanded spectrum of values and criteria for measuring organizational success: economic, ecological and social. With the ratification of the United Nations and ICLEI _________ standard for urban and community accounting in early 2007, this became the dominant approach to public sector full cost accounting. Similar UN standards apply to natural capital and human capital measurement to assist in measurements required by _________, e.g. the ecoBudget standard for reporting ecological footprint.

a. 1990 Clean Air Act
b. 33 Strategies of War
c. 28-hour day
d. Triple bottom line

2. In game theory, an _________ is a set of moves or strategies taken by the players, or their payoffs resulting from the actions or strategies taken by all players. The two are complementary in that given knowledge of the set of strategies of all players, the final state of the game is known, as are any relevant payoffs. In a game where chance or a random event is involved, the _________ is not known from only the set of strategies, but is only realized when the random event(s) are realized.

a. AAAI
b. A4e
c. Outcome
d. A Stake in the Outcome

3. _________ is a civil designation for persons who are incorporated in a fixed or permanent way to a society or group: regular member of the working staff, permanent staff distinguished from a supernumerary.

The term '_________' and its counterpart, 'supernumerary,' originated in Spanish and Latin American academy and government; it is now also used in countries all over the world, such as France, the U.S., England, Italy, etc.

There are _________ members of surgical organizations, of universities, of gastronomical associations, etc.

a. Adam Smith
b. Affiliation
c. Numerary
d. Abraham Harold Maslow

4. _________ involves establishing specific, measurable and time-targeted objectives. Work on the theory of goal-setting suggests that it's an effective tool for making progress by ensuring that participants in a group with a common goal are clearly aware of what is expected from them if an objective is to be achieved. On a personal level, setting goals is a process that allows people to specify then work towards their own objectives - most commonly with financial or career-based goals.

a. Digital strategy
b. Catfish effect
c. Resource-based view
d. Goal setting

5. _________ is a process of agreeing upon objectives within an organization so that management and employees agree to the objectives and understand what they are in the organization.

The term '_________' was first popularized by Peter Drucker in his 1954 book 'The Practice of Management'.

The essence of _________ is participative goal setting, choosing course of actions and decision making.

a. Business economics
b. Job enrichment
c. Clean sheet review
d. Management by objectives

6. In statistics, _________ is:

- the arithmetic _________
- the expected value of a random variable, which is also called the population _________.

It is sometimes stated that the '_________' _________s average. This is incorrect if '_________' is taken in the specific sense of 'arithmetic _________' as there are different types of averages: the _________, median, and mode. Other simple statistical analyses use measures of spread, such as range, interquartile range, or standard deviation. For a real-valued random variable X, the _________ is the expectation of X. Note that not every probability distribution has a defined _________; see the Cauchy distribution for an example.

a. Statistical inference
b. Correlation
c. Control chart
d. Mean

1. _________ is a strategic planning method used to evaluate the Strengths, Weaknesses, Opportunities, and Threats involved in a project or in a business venture. It involves specifying the objective of the business venture or project and identifying the internal and external factors that are favorable and unfavorable to achieving that objective. The technique is credited to Albert Humphrey, who led a convention at Stanford University in the 1960s and 1970s using data from Fortune 500 companies.

a. SWOT analysis
b. Marketing
c. Market share
d. Corporate image

2. A _________ is a framework for creating economic, social, and/or other forms of value. The term _________ is thus used for a broad range of informal and formal descriptions to represent core aspects of a business, including purpose, offerings, strategies, infrastructure, organizational structures, trading practices, and operational processes and policies.

Conceptualizations of _________s try to formalize informal descriptions into building blocks and their relationships.

a. Business model
b. Business model design
c. Business networking
d. Gap analysis

3. _________ is a process of planning and controlling the performance or execution of any type of activity, such as:

- a project (project _________) or
- a process (process _________, sometimes referred to as the process performance measurement and management system.)

Organization's senior management is responsible for carrying out its _________.

a. Management process
b. Participatory management
c. Work design
d. Human Relations Movement

4. _________ is an organization's process of defining its strategy and making decisions on allocating its resources to pursue this strategy, including its capital and people. Various business analysis techniques can be used in _________, including SWOT analysis (Strengths, Weaknesses, Opportunities, and Threats) and PEST analysis (Political, Economic, Social, and Technological analysis) or STEER analysis involving Socio-cultural, Technological, Economic, Ecological, and Regulatory factors and EPISTEL (Environment, Political, Informatic, Social, Technological, Economic and Legal)

_________ is the formal consideration of an organization's future course. All _________ deals with at least one of three key questions:

1. 'What do we do?'
2. 'For whom do we do it?'
3. 'How do we excel?'

In business _________, the third question is better phrased 'How can we beat or avoid competition?'. (Bradford and Duncan, page 1.)

a. 33 Strategies of War
b. 1990 Clean Air Act
c. Strategic planning
d. 28-hour day

5. _________ is something that a firm can do well and that meets the following three conditions:

Competencies are things that companys execute well across several business units or product sectors.

Firms usually have few competencies, but these are usually less liable to change rapidly.

1. It provides consumer benefits
2. It is not easy for competitors to imitate
3. It can be leveraged widely to many products and markets.

A _________ can take various forms, including technical/subject matter know-how, a reliable process and/or close relationships with customers and suppliers (Mascarenhas et al. 1998.)

a. NAIRU
b. Core competency
c. Learning-by-doing
d. Dominant Design

6. In business and accounting, _________s are everything of value that is owned by a person or company. Any property or object of value that one possesses, usually considered as applicable to the payment of one's debts is considered an _________. Simplistically stated, _________s are things of value that can be readily converted into cash.

a. AAAI
b. A4e
c. Asset
d. A Stake in the Outcome

7. _________ is an advertisement in which a particular product specifically mentions a competitor by name for the express purpose of showing why the competitor is inferior to the product naming it.

This should not be confused with parody advertisements, where a fictional product is being advertised for the purpose of poking fun at the particular advertisement, nor should it be confused with the use of a coined brand name for the purpose of comparing the product without actually naming an actual competitor. ('Wikipedia tastes better and is less filling than the Encyclopedia Galactica.')

In the 1980s, during what has been referred to as the cola wars, soft-drink manufacturer Pepsi ran a series of advertisements where people, caught on hidden camera, in a blind taste test, chose Pepsi over rival Coca-Cola.

a. 28-hour day
b. 1990 Clean Air Act
c. 33 Strategies of War
d. Comparative advertising

8. The term '_________' refers to the concept of collecting information and attempting to spot a pattern in the information. In some fields of study, the term '_________' has more formally-defined meanings.

In project management _________ is a mathematical technique that uses historical results to predict future outcome.

a. Stepwise regression
b. Regression analysis
c. Least squares
d. Trend analysis

9. _________ is an idea in the field of Organizational studies and management which describes the psychology, attitudes, experiences, beliefs and Values (personal and cultural values) of an organization. It has been defined as 'the specific collection of values and norms that are shared by people and groups in an organization and that control the way they interact with each other and with stakeholders outside the organization.'

This definition continues to explain organizational values also known as 'beliefs and ideas about what kinds of goals members of an organization should pursue and ideas about the appropriate kinds or standards of behavior organizational members should use to achieve these goals. From organizational values develop organizational norms, guidelines or expectations that prescribe appropriate kinds of behavior by employees in particular situations and control the behavior of organizational members towards one another.'

_________ is not the same as corporate culture.

a. Organizational effectiveness
b. Organizational development
c. Union shop
d. Organizational culture

10. _________ is a civil designation for persons who are incorporated in a fixed or permanent way to a society or group: regular member of the working staff, permanent staff distinguished from a supernumerary.

The term '_________' and its counterpart, 'supernumerary,' originated in Spanish and Latin American academy and government; it is now also used in countries all over the world, such as France, the U.S., England, Italy, etc.

There are _________ members of surgical organizations, of universities, of gastronomical associations, etc.

a. Affiliation
b. Abraham Harold Maslow
c. Numerary
d. Adam Smith

11. _________ refers to the overarching strategy of the diversified firm. Such a _________ answers the questions of 'in which businesses should we be in?' and 'how does being in these business create synergy and/or add to the competitive advantage of the corporation as a whole?'

Business strategy refers to the aggregated strategies of single business firm or a strategic business unit (SBU) in a diversified corporation. According to Michael Porter, a firm must formulate a business strategy that incorporates either cost leadership, differentiation or focus in order to achieve a sustainable competitive advantage and long-term success in its chosen arenas or industries.

a. Competitive heterogeneity
b. Strategic group
c. Strategic drift
d. Corporate strategy

12. A _________ is a process in which a potential employee is evaluated by an employer for prospective employment in their company, organization and was established in the late 16th century.

A _________ typically precedes the hiring decision, and is used to evaluate the candidate. The interview is usually preceded by the evaluation of submitted résumés from interested candidates, then selecting a small number of candidates for interviews.

a. Supported employment
b. Payrolling
c. Split shift
d. Job interview

13. In microeconomics and strategic management, the term _________ describes a type of ownership and control. It is a strategy used by a business or corporation that seeks to sell a type of product in numerous markets. _________ in marketing is much more common than vertical integration is in production.

a. Farmshoring
b. Career development
c. No-bid contract
d. Horizontal integration

14. The _________ is a chart that had been created by Bruce Henderson for the Boston Consulting Group in 1970 to help corporations with analyzing their business units or product lines. This helps the company allocate resources and is used as an analytical tool in brand marketing, product management, strategic management, and portfolio analysis. _________

To use the chart, analysts plot a scatter graph to rank the business units (or products) on the basis of their relative market shares and growth rates.

a. BCG matrix
b. Marketing strategy
c. Marketing plan
d. Market segment

15. In business, a _________ is a product or a business unit that generates unusually high profit margins: so high that it is responsible for a large amount of a company's operating profit. This profit far exceeds the amount necessary to maintain the _________ business, and the excess is used by the business for other purposes.

A firm is said to be acting as a _________ when its earnings per share (EPS) is equal to its dividends per share (DPS), or in other words, when a firm pays out 100% of its free cash flow (FCF) to its shareholders as dividends at the end of each accounting term.

a. Cash cow
b. Workflow
c. Middle management
d. Design management in organization

16. _________, in strategic management and marketing is, according to Carlton O'Neal, the percentage or proportion of the total available market or market segment that is being serviced by a company. It can be expressed as a company's sales revenue (from that market) divided by the total sales revenue available in that market. It can also be expressed as a company's unit sales volume (in a market) divided by the total volume of units sold in that market.
a. Business-to-business
b. Marketing plan
c. Market share
d. Green marketing

17. _________ is a forward looking process for setting goals and regularly checking progress toward achieving those goals. It is a continual feedback process whereby the actual outputs are measured and compared with the desired goals. Any discrepancy or gap is then fed back into changing the inputs of the process, so as to achieve the desired goals or outputs.
a. 33 Strategies of War
b. 28-hour day
c. 1990 Clean Air Act
d. Performance management

18. _________ is used to assign the available resources in an economic way. It is part of resource management.

In strategic planning,is a plan for using available resources, for example human resources, especially in the near term, to achieve goals for the future.

a. 28-hour day
b. 33 Strategies of War
c. 1990 Clean Air Act
d. Resource allocation

19. _________ refers to the aggregated strategies of single business firm or a strategic business unit (SBU) in a diversified corporation. According to Michael Porter, a firm must formulate a _________ that incorporates either cost leadership, differentiation or focus in order to achieve a sustainable competitive advantage and long-term success in its chosen arenas or industries.

Functional strategies include marketing strategies, new product development strategies, human resource strategies, financial strategies, legal strategies, supply-chain strategies, and information technology management strategies.

a. Competitive heterogeneity
b. Strategic thinking
c. Switching cost
d. Business strategy

20. The _________ (Situation, Task, Action, Result) format is a job interview technique used by interviewers to gather all the relevant information about a specific capability that the job requires. This interview format is said to have a higher degree of predictability of future on-the-job performance than the traditional interview.

- Situation: The interviewer wants you to present a recent challenge and situation in which you found yourself.
- Task: What did you have to achieve? The interviewer will be looking to see what you were trying to achieve from the situation.
- Action: What did you do? The interviewer will be looking for information on what you did, why you did it and what were the alternatives.
- Results: What was the outcome of your actions? What did you achieve through your actions and did you meet your objectives. What did you learn from this experience and have you used this learning since?

.

a. Competency-based job descriptions
b. Star
c. Phrase completion
d. Rasch models

21. _________ is, in very basic words, a position a firm occupies against its competitors.

According to Michael Porter, the three methods for creating a sustainable _________ are through:

1. Cost leadership

2. Differentiation

3. Focus (economics)

a. Theory Z
b. 28-hour day
c. 1990 Clean Air Act
d. Competitive advantage

22. _________ can be considered to have three main components: quality control, quality assurance and quality improvement. _________ is focused not only on product quality, but also the means to achieve it. _________ therefore uses quality assurance and control of processes as well as products to achieve more consistent quality.

a. Total quality management
b. 1990 Clean Air Act
c. 28-hour day
d. Quality management

23. _________ is understood as a business unit within the overall corporate identity which is distinguishable from other business because it serves a defined external market where management can conduct strategic planning in relation to products and markets. When companies become really large, they are best thought of as being composed of a number of businesses (or _________s.)

In the broader domain of strategic management, the phrase '_________' came into use in the 1960s, largely as a result of General Electric's many units.

a. Switching cost
b. Strategic group
c. Strategic drift
d. Strategic business unit

24. _________ is a process or productivity improvement tool intended to have a stable and consistent growth and improvement of all the segments of a process or processes. _________ ensures the process stabilization and further improvement. When an organization's growth and development is intended, identification of all the processes and development of a measurement analysis of each process step is necessary.

a. 28-hour day
b. 33 Strategies of War
c. 1990 Clean Air Act
d. Continual improvement

25. In economics, business, retail, and accounting, a _________ is the value of money that has been used up to produce something, and hence is not available for use anymore. In economics, a _________ is an alternative that is given up as a result of a decision. In business, the _________ may be one of acquisition, in which case the amount of money expended to acquire it is counted as _________.

a. Fixed costs
b. Cost allocation
c. Cost overrun
d. Cost

26. _________ is a concept developed by Michael Porter, used in business strategy. It describes a way to establish the competitive advantage. _________, in basic words, means the lowest cost of operation in the industry.

a. Strategic group
b. Cost leadership
c. Switching cost
d. Strategic business unit

27. _________ has been described as the 'process of social influence in which one person can enlist the aid and support of others in the accomplishment of a common task' . A definition more inclusive of followers comes from Alan Keith of Genentech who said '_________ is ultimately about creating a way for people to contribute to making something extraordinary happen.'

_________ is one of the most salient aspects of the organizational context. However, defining _________ has been challenging.

a. 1990 Clean Air Act
b. 28-hour day
c. Leadership
d. Situational leadership

28. _________ is the provision of service to customers before, during and after a purchase.

According to Turban et al. (2002), '_________ is a series of activities designed to enhance the level of customer satisfaction - that is, the feeling that a product or service has met the customer expectation.'

Its importance varies by product, industry and customer; defective or broken merchandise can be exchanged, often only with a receipt and within a specified time frame.

a. 1990 Clean Air Act
b. Service rate
c. 28-hour day
d. Customer service

29. _________, commonly referred to as 'eBusiness' or 'e-Business', may be defined as the utilization of information and communication technologies (ICT) in support of all the activities of business. Commerce constitutes the exchange of products and services between businesses, groups and individuals and hence can be seen as one of the essential activities of any business. Hence, electronic commerce or eCommerce focuses on the use of ICT to enable the external activities and relationships of the business with individuals, groups and other businesses .

a. A4e
b. A Stake in the Outcome
c. AAAI
d. Electronic business

30. _________ is the advantage gained by the initial occupant of a market segment. This advantage may stem from the fact that the first entrant can gain control of resources that followers may not be able to match. Sometimes the first mover is not able to capitalise on its advantage, leaving the opportunity for another firm to gain second-mover advantage.

a. Horizontal integration
b. Customer retention
c. Business ecosystem
d. First-mover advantage

31. In business and engineering, new _________ is the term used to describe the complete process of bringing a new product or service to market. There are two parallel paths involved in the NProduct development process: one involves the idea generation, product design, and detail engineering; the other involves market research and marketing analysis. Companies typically see new _________ as the first stage in generating and commercializing new products within the overall strategic process of product life cycle management used to maintain or grow their market share.

a. Product development
b. 33 Strategies of War
c. 1990 Clean Air Act
d. 28-hour day

32. The process of _________ involves the introduction of a good or service that is new or substantially improved. This includes, but is not limited to, improvements in functional characteristics, technical abilities, or ease of use.

a. Product innovation
b. Service-profit chain
c. Job enlargement
d. Letter of resignation

1. _________ is a process of gathering, analyzing, and dispensing information for tactical or strategic purposes. The _________ process entails obtaining both factual and subjective information on the business environments in which a company is operating or considering entering.

There are three ways of scanning the business environment:

- Ad-hoc scanning - Short term, infrequent examinations usually initiated by a crisis
- Regular scanning - Studies done on a regular schedule (say, once a year)
- Continuous scanning(also called continuous learning) - continuous structured data collection and processing on a broad range of environmental factors

Most commentators feel that in today's turbulent business environment the best scanning method available is continuous scanning. This allows the firm to :

-act quickly-take advantage of opportunities before competitors do-respond to environmental threats before significant damage is done

a. A4e
b. AAAI
c. A Stake in the Outcome
d. Environmental scanning

2. _________ is the original form of externally-oriented business intelligence that preceded Knowledge Management or Data Mining as the primary concern of executives responsible for increasing market share.
a. 1990 Clean Air Act
b. 28-hour day
c. Competitor analysis
d. Competitor or Competitive Intelligence

3. _________ is the process of discovering the technological principles of a device, object or system through analysis of its structure, function and operation. It often involves taking something (e.g., a mechanical device, electronic component, or software program) apart and analyzing its workings in detail to be used in maintenance, or to try to make a new device or program that does the same thing without copying anything from the original.

_________ has its origins in the analysis of hardware for commercial or military advantage .

a. 1990 Clean Air Act
b. 28-hour day
c. Predictive maintenance
d. Reverse engineering

4. The _________ of 1996 (18 U.S.C. Â§ 1831-1839) makes the theft or misappropriation of a trade secret a federal crime. Unlike Espionage, which is governed by Title 18 U.S. Code Sections 792 - 799, the offense involves commercial information, not classified or national defense information.

a. Economic Espionage Act
b. A4e
c. A Stake in the Outcome
d. AAAI

5. _________ is the process of estimation in unknown situations. Prediction is a similar, but more general term. Both can refer to estimation of time series, cross-sectional or longitudinal data.

a. Forecasting
b. 28-hour day
c. 1990 Clean Air Act
d. 33 Strategies of War

6. In game theory, an _________ is a set of moves or strategies taken by the players, or their payoffs resulting from the actions or strategies taken by all players. The two are complementary in that given knowledge of the set of strategies of all players, the final state of the game is known, as are any relevant payoffs. In a game where chance or a random event is involved, the _________ is not known from only the set of strategies, but is only realized when the random event(s) are realized.

a. AAAI
b. A4e
c. A Stake in the Outcome
d. Outcome

7. _________ is the process of comparing the cost, cycle time, productivity, or quality of a specific process or method to another that is widely considered to be an industry standard or best practice. Essentially, _________ provides a snapshot of the performance of your business and helps you understand where you are in relation to a particular standard. The result is often a business case for making changes in order to make improvements.

a. Cost leadership
b. Competitive heterogeneity
c. Complementors
d. Benchmarking

8. A _________ is the belief that there is a technique, method, process, activity, incentive or reward that is more effective at delivering a particular outcome than any other technique, method, process, etc. The idea is that with proper processes, checks, and testing, a desired outcome can be delivered with fewer problems and unforeseen complications. _________s can also be defined as the most efficient (least amount of effort) and effective (best results) way of accomplishing a task, based on repeatable procedures that have proven themselves over time for large numbers of people.
   a. Fix it twice
   b. Design management
   c. Hierarchical organization
   d. Best practice

9. _________ generally refers to a list of all planned expenses and revenues. It is a plan for saving and spending. A _________ is an important concept in microeconomics, which uses a _________ line to illustrate the trade-offs between two or more goods.
   a. 33 Strategies of War
   b. 1990 Clean Air Act
   c. Budget
   d. 28-hour day

10. _________ is used to assign the available resources in an economic way. It is part of resource management.

In strategic planning,is a plan for using available resources, for example human resources, especially in the near term, to achieve goals for the future.

   a. 33 Strategies of War
   b. 1990 Clean Air Act
   c. 28-hour day
   d. Resource allocation

11. In business and accounting, _________s are everything of value that is owned by a person or company. Any property or object of value that one possesses, usually considered as applicable to the payment of one's debts is considered an _________. Simplistically stated, _________s are things of value that can be readily converted into cash.
   a. AAAI
   b. Asset
   c. A4e
   d. A Stake in the Outcome

12. _________ is an advertisement in which a particular product specifically mentions a competitor by name for the express purpose of showing why the competitor is inferior to the product naming it.

This should not be confused with parody advertisements, where a fictional product is being advertised for the purpose of poking fun at the particular advertisement, nor should it be confused with the use of a coined brand name for the purpose of comparing the product without actually naming an actual competitor. ('Wikipedia tastes better and is less filling than the Encyclopedia Galactica.')

In the 1980s, during what has been referred to as the cola wars, soft-drink manufacturer Pepsi ran a series of advertisements where people, caught on hidden camera, in a blind taste test, chose Pepsi over rival Coca-Cola.

a. 28-hour day
b. 33 Strategies of War
c. 1990 Clean Air Act
d. Comparative advertising

13. A _________ is a type of bar chart that illustrates a project schedule. _________s illustrate the start and finish dates of the terminal elements and summary elements of a project. Terminal elements and summary elements comprise the work breakdown structure of the project.
a. 28-hour day
b. 1990 Clean Air Act
c. 33 Strategies of War
d. Gantt chart

14. The Program (or Project) Evaluation and Review Technique, commonly abbreviated _________, is a model for project management designed to analyze and represent the tasks involved in completing a given project.

_________ is a method to analyze the involved tasks in completing a given project, specially the time needed to complete each task, and identifying the minimum time needed to complete the total project.

_________ was developed primarily to simplify the planning and scheduling of large and complex projects.

a. 1990 Clean Air Act
b. 28-hour day
c. 33 Strategies of War
d. PERT

15. In economics, business, retail, and accounting, a _________ is the value of money that has been used up to produce something, and hence is not available for use anymore. In economics, a _________ is an alternative that is given up as a result of a decision. In business, the _________ may be one of acquisition, in which case the amount of money expended to acquire it is counted as _________.

a. Cost
b. Fixed costs
c. Cost allocation
d. Cost overrun

16. A _________ is a common type of chart, that represents an algorithm or process, showing the steps as boxes of various kinds, and their order by connecting these with arrows. _________s are used in analyzing, designing, documenting or managing a process or program in various fields.

The first structured method for documenting process flow, the 'flow process chart', was introduced by Frank Gilbreth to members of ASME in 1921 as the presentation 'Process Charts--First Steps in Finding the One Best Way'.

a. 28-hour day
b. 33 Strategies of War
c. 1990 Clean Air Act
d. Flowchart

17. _________ refers to the movement of cash into or out of a business or financial product. It is usually measured during a specified, finite period of time. Measurement of _________ can be used

- to determine a project's rate of return or value. The time of _________s into and out of projects are used as inputs in financial models such as internal rate of return, and net present value.
- to determine problems with a business's liquidity. Being profitable does not necessarily mean being liquid. A company can fail because of a shortage of cash, even while profitable.
- as an alternate measure of a business's profits when it is believed that accrual accounting concepts do not represent economic realities. For example, a company may be notionally profitable but generating little operational cash (as may be the case for a company that barters its products rather than selling for cash.) In such a case, the company may be deriving additional operating cash by issuing shares evaluating default risk, re-investment requirements, etc.

_________ is a generic term used differently depending on the context. It may be defined by users for their own purposes.

a. Sweat equity
b. Gross profit margin
c. Cash flow
d. Gross profit

18. _________s are expenses that change in proportion to the activity of a business. In other words, _________ is the sum of marginal costs. It can also be considered normal costs.

a. Cost accounting
b. Cost overrun
c. Fixed costs
d. Variable cost

19. In economics, _________ are business expenses that are not dependent on the activities of the business They tend to be time-related, such as salaries or rents being paid per month. This is in contrast to variable costs, which are volume-related (and are paid per quantity.)

In management accounting, _________ are defined as expenses that do not change in proportion to the activity of a business, within the relevant period or scale of production.

a. Cost of quality
b. Fixed costs
c. Cost allocation
d. Transaction cost

20. In economics, and cost accounting, _________ describes the total economic cost of production and is made up of variable costs, which vary according to the quantity of a good produced and include inputs such as labor and raw materials, plus fixed costs, which are independent of the quantity of a good produced and include inputs (capital) that cannot be varied in the short term, such as buildings and machinery. _________ in economics includes the total opportunity cost of each factor of production in addition to fixed and variable costs.

The rate at which _________ changes as the amount produced changes is called marginal cost.

a. 28-hour day
b. 1990 Clean Air Act
c. 33 Strategies of War
d. Total cost

21. In mathematics, _________ is a technique for optimization of a linear objective function, subject to linear equality and linear inequality constraints. Informally, _________ determines the way to achieve the best outcome (such as maximum profit or lowest cost) in a given mathematical model and given some list of requirements represented as linear equations.

More formally, given a polytope (for example, a polygon or a polyhedron), and a real-valued affine function

$$f(x_1, x_2, \dots, x_n) = c_1 x_1 + c_2 x_2 + \cdots + c_n x_n + d$$

defined on this polytope, a _________ method will find a point in the polytope where this function has the smallest (or largest) value.

a. Linear programming relaxation
b. Linear programming
c. 1990 Clean Air Act
d. Slack variable

22. The function f is called, variously, an _________, cost function, energy function, or energy functional. A feasible solution that minimizes (or maximizes, if that is the goal) the _________ is called an optimal solution.

Generally, when the feasible region or the _________ of the problem does not present convexity, there may be several local minima and maxima, where a local minimum x^* is defined as a point for which there exists some >δ > 0 so that for all x such that

>

the expression

>

holds; that is to say, on some region around x^* all of the function values are greater than or equal to the value at that point.

a. A4e
b. A Stake in the Outcome
c. AAAI
d. Objective function

23. _________ is the discipline of planning, organizing and managing resources to bring about the successful completion of specific project goals and objectives. It is often closely related to and sometimes conflated with Program management.

A project is a finite endeavor--having specific start and completion dates--undertaken to meet particular goals and objectives, usually to bring about beneficial change or added value.

a. Project management
b. Project engineer
c. Work package
d. Precedence diagram

24. _________ is a strategic planning method that some organizations use to make flexible long-term plans. It is in large part an adaptation and generalization of classic methods used by military intelligence.

The original method was that a group of analysts would generate simulation games for policy makers. In business applications, the emphasis on gaming the behavior of opponents was reduced (shifting more toward a game against nature). At Royal Dutch/Shell for example, _________ was viewed as changing mindsets about the exogenous part of the world, prior to formulating specific strategies.

a. Time and attendance
b. Labour productivity
c. Retroactive overtime
d. Scenario Planning

1. An _________ is a mostly hierarchical concept of subordination of entities that collaborate and contribute to serve one common aim.

Organizations are a variant of clustered entities. The structure of an organization is usually set up in many a styles, dependent on their objectives and ambience.

a. Organizational development
b. Organizational structure
c. Informal organization
d. Open shop

2. A _________ is a group of employees from various functional areas of the organization - research, engineering, marketing, finance. human resources, and operations, for example - who are all focused on a specific objective and are responsible to work as a team to improve coordination and innovation across divisions and resolve mutual problems.
a. Goal-setting theory
b. Sociotechnical systems
c. Graduate recruitment
d. Cross-functional team

3. _________ refers to the process of grouping activities into departments.

Division of labour creates specialists who need coordination. This coordination is facilitated by grouping specialists together in departments.

a. Decent work
b. Maximum wage
c. Division of labour
d. Departmentalization

4. In a military context, the _________ is the line of authority and responsibility along which orders are passed within a military unit and between different units. The term is also used in a civilian management context describing comparable hierarchical structures of authority.
a. French leave
b. 28-hour day
c. 1990 Clean Air Act
d. Chain of command

5. A _________ is a list of the general tasks and responsibilities of a position. Typically, it also includes to whom the position reports, specifications such as the qualifications needed by the person in the job, salary range for the position, etc. A _________ is usually developed by conducting a job analysis, which includes examining the tasks and sequences of tasks necessary to perform the job.
   a. Recruitment
   b. Recruitment advertising
   c. Recruitment Process Insourcing
   d. Job description

6. There are many important decisions about product and service development and marketing. In the process of product development and marketing we should focus on strategic decisions about product attributes, product branding, product packaging, product labeling and product support services. But product strategy also calls for building a _________.
   a. Context analysis
   b. Product line
   c. Product bundling
   d. Marketing strategy

7. _________ is a term originating in military organization theory, but now used more commonly in business management, particularly human resource management. _________ refers to the number of subordinates a supervisor has.

In the hierarchical business organization of the past it was not uncommon to see average spans of 1 to 10 or even less. That is, one manager supervised ten employees on average.

   a. Senior management
   b. CIFMS
   c. Span of control
   d. Mentoring

8. The _________ is a standardized, on-scene, all-hazard incident management concept. It is a management protocol originally designed for emergency management agencies in the United States which was later federalized there. It has since been adopted by agencies in other countries.
   a. A Stake in the Outcome
   b. A4e
   c. AAAI
   d. Incident Command Structure

9. _________ is one of the managerial functions like planning, organizing, staffing and directing. It is an important function because it helps to check the errors and to take the corrective action so that deviation from standards are minimized and stated goals of the organization are achieved in desired manner.According to modern concepts, _________ is a foreseeing action whereas earlier concept of _________ was used only when errors were detected. _________ in management means setting standards, measuring actual performance and taking corrective action.

a. Decision tree pruning
b. Schedule of reinforcement
c. Turnover
d. Control

10. The _________ captures an expanded spectrum of values and criteria for measuring organizational success: economic, ecological and social. With the ratification of the United Nations and ICLEI _________ standard for urban and community accounting in early 2007, this became the dominant approach to public sector full cost accounting. Similar UN standards apply to natural capital and human capital measurement to assist in measurements required by _________, e.g. the ecoBudget standard for reporting ecological footprint.

a. 28-hour day
b. 1990 Clean Air Act
c. 33 Strategies of War
d. Triple bottom line

11. _________ is the process by which the activities of an organisation, particularly those regarding decision-making, become concentrated within a particular location and/or group.

a. Chief operating officer
b. Corner office
c. Product innovation
d. Centralization

12. _________ is the process of dispersing decision-making governance closer to the people or citizen. It includes the dispersal of administration or governance in sectors or areas like engineering, management science, political science, political economy, sociology and economics. _________ is also possible in the dispersal of population and employment.

a. Decentralization
b. Business plan
c. Frenemy
d. Formula for Change

13. _________ can be regarded as an outcome of mental processes (cognitive process) leading to the selection of a course of action among several alternatives. Every _________ process produces a final choice. The output can be an action or an opinion of choice.

a. 33 Strategies of War
b. 1990 Clean Air Act
c. Decision making
d. 28-hour day

14. A chief executive officer (_________) or chief executive is one of the highest-ranking corporate officer (executive) or administrator in charge of total management. An individual selected as President and _________ of a corporation, company, organization, or agency, reports to the board of directors. In internal communication and press releases, many companies capitalize the term and those of other high positions, even when they are not proper nouns.
a. CEO
b. Chief executive officer
c. Director of communications
d. Portfolio manager

15. _________ refers to increasing the spiritual, political, social or economic strength of individuals and communities. It often involves the empowered developing confidence in their own capacities.

The term Human _________ covers a vast landscape of meanings, interpretations, definitions and disciplines ranging from psychology and philosophy to the highly commercialized Self-Help industry and Motivational sciences.

a. Empowerment
b. AAAI
c. A Stake in the Outcome
d. A4e

16. _________ is the production of large amounts of standardized products, including and especially on assembly lines. The concepts of _________ are applied to various kinds of products, from fluids and particulates handled in bulk to discrete solid parts to assemblies of such parts

_________ of assemblies typically uses electric-motor-powered moving tracks or conveyor belts to move partially complete products to workers, who perform simple repetitive tasks.

a. 33 Strategies of War
b. 1990 Clean Air Act
c. 28-hour day
d. Mass production

17. In probability theory, a probability distribution is called _________ if its cumulative distribution function is _________. This is equivalent to saying that for random variables X with the distribution in question, Pr[X = a] = 0 for all real numbers a, i.e.: the probability that X attains the value a is zero, for any number a. If the distribution of X is _________ then X is called a _________ random variable.

a. Pay Band
b. Connectionist expert systems
c. Continuous
d. Decision tree pruning

18. The 'business case for _________', theorizes that in a global marketplace, a company that employs a diverse workforce (both men and women, people of many generations, people from ethnically and racially diverse backgrounds etc.) is better able to understand the demographics of the marketplace it serves and is thus better equipped to thrive in that marketplace than a company that has a more limited range of employee demographics.

An additional corollary suggests that a company that supports the _________ of its workforce can also improve employee satisfaction, productivity and retention.

a. Kanban
b. Virtual team
c. Trademark
d. Diversity

19. _________ refers to the movement of cash into or out of a business or financial product. It is usually measured during a specified, finite period of time. Measurement of _________ can be used

- to determine a project's rate of return or value. The time of _________s into and out of projects are used as inputs in financial models such as internal rate of return, and net present value.
- to determine problems with a business's liquidity. Being profitable does not necessarily mean being liquid. A company can fail because of a shortage of cash, even while profitable.
- as an alternate measure of a business's profits when it is believed that accrual accounting concepts do not represent economic realities. For example, a company may be notionally profitable but generating little operational cash (as may be the case for a company that barters its products rather than selling for cash.) In such a case, the company may be deriving additional operating cash by issuing shares evaluating default risk, re-investment requirements, etc.

_________ is a generic term used differently depending on the context. It may be defined by users for their own purposes.

a. Gross profit
b. Gross profit margin
c. Cash flow
d. Sweat equity

20. A _________ is a contemporary apporach to organizational design. It is an organization that is not defined by, or limited to, the horizontal, vertical, or external boundaries imposed by a predefined structure. This term was coined by former GE chairman Jack Welch because he wanted to eliminate vertical and horizontal boundaries within GE and break down external barriers between the company and its customers and suppliers.
a. Headquarters
b. Chief risk officer
c. Boundaryless organization
d. Business Roundtable

21. _________ is 'interfirm coordination that is characterized by organic or informal social systems, in contrast to bureaucratic structures within firms and formal contractual relationships between them.(Gerlach, 1992:64; Nohria, 1992)' A useful survey of network organization theory appears in Van Alstyne (1997).

The concepts of privatization, public private partnership, and contracting are defined in this context.

As a concept, _________ explains increased efficiency and reduced agency problems for organizations existing in highly turbulent environments . Due to the rapid pace of modern society and competitive pressures from globalization, _________ has gained prominence and development among sociological theorists. As a concept, _________ explains increased efficiency and reduced agency problems for organizations existing in highly turbulent environments.

a. Network governance
b. 33 Strategies of War
c. 28-hour day
d. 1990 Clean Air Act

22. A _________ is the term given to a company that facilitates the learning of its members and continuously transforms itself. _________s develop as a result of the pressures facing modern organizations and enables them to remain competitive in the business environment. A _________ has five main features; systems thinking, personal mastery, mental models, shared vision and team learning.

a. Hoshin Kanri
b. 1990 Clean Air Act
c. Quality function deployment
d. Learning organization

23. _________, e-commuting, e-work, telework, working from home (WFH), or working at home (WAH) is a work arrangement in which employees enjoy flexibility in working location and hours. In other words, the daily commute to a central place of work is replaced by telecommunication links. Many work from home, while others, occasionally also referred to as nomad workers or web commuters utilize mobile telecommunications technology to work from coffee shops or myriad other locations.

a. 28-hour day
b. 33 Strategies of War
c. Telecommuting
d. 1990 Clean Air Act

1. A _________ is a list of the general tasks and responsibilities of a position. Typically, it also includes to whom the position reports, specifications such as the qualifications needed by the person in the job, salary range for the position, etc. A _________ is usually developed by conducting a job analysis, which includes examining the tasks and sequences of tasks necessary to perform the job.

a. Recruitment Process Insourcing
b. Recruitment
c. Recruitment advertising
d. Job description

2. _________ is a subfield of the larger discipline of communication studies. _________, as a field, is the consideration, analysis, and criticism of the role of communication in organizational contexts.

The field traces its lineage through business information, business communication, and early mass communication studies published in the 1930s through the 1950s.

a. Organizational communication
b. A4e
c. AAAI
d. A Stake in the Outcome

3. The _________ captures an expanded spectrum of values and criteria for measuring organizational success: economic, ecological and social. With the ratification of the United Nations and ICLEI _________ standard for urban and community accounting in early 2007, this became the dominant approach to public sector full cost accounting. Similar UN standards apply to natural capital and human capital measurement to assist in measurements required by _________, e.g. the ecoBudget standard for reporting ecological footprint.

a. 33 Strategies of War
b. 28-hour day
c. Triple bottom line
d. 1990 Clean Air Act

4. _________ describes the situation when output from (or information about the result of) an event or phenomenon in the past will influence the same event/phenomenon in the present or future. When an event is part of a chain of cause-and-effect that forms a circuit or loop, then the event is said to 'feed back' into itself.

_________ is also a synonym for:

- _________ signal; the information about the initial event that is the basis for subsequent modification of the event.
- _________ loop; the causal path that leads from the initial generation of the _________ signal to the subsequent modification of the event.

_________ is a mechanism, process or signal that is looped back to control a system within itself. Such a loop is called a _________ loop.

a. Positive feedback
b. 1990 Clean Air Act
c. Feedback
d. Feedback loop

5. Feedback describes the situation when output from (or information about the result of) an event or phenomenon in the past will influence the same event/phenomenon in the present or future. When an event is part of a chain of cause-and-effect that forms a circuit or loop, then the event is said to 'feed back' into itself.

Feedback is also a synonym for:

- Feedback signal; the information about the initial event that is the basis for subsequent modification of the event.
- _________; the causal path that leads from the initial generation of the feedback signal to the subsequent modification of the event.

Feedback is a mechanism, process or signal that is looped back to control a system within itself. Such a loop is called a _________.

a. Negative feedback
b. Positive feedback
c. 1990 Clean Air Act
d. Feedback loop

6. The 'business case for _________', theorizes that in a global marketplace, a company that employs a diverse workforce (both men and women, people of many generations, people from ethnically and racially diverse backgrounds etc.) is better able to understand the demographics of the marketplace it serves and is thus better equipped to thrive in that marketplace than a company that has a more limited range of employee demographics.

An additional corollary suggests that a company that supports the _________ of its workforce can also improve employee satisfaction, productivity and retention.

a. Diversity
b. Virtual team
c. Trademark
d. Kanban

7. _________ is a civil designation for persons who are incorporated in a fixed or permanent way to a society or group: regular member of the working staff, permanent staff distinguished from a supernumerary.

The term '_________' and its counterpart, 'supernumerary,' originated in Spanish and Latin American academy and government; it is now also used in countries all over the world, such as France, the U.S., England, Italy, etc.

There are _________ members of surgical organizations, of universities, of gastronomical associations, etc.

a. Adam Smith
b. Abraham Harold Maslow
c. Numerary
d. Affiliation

8. The _________ is the labour pool in employment. It is generally used to describe those working for a single company or industry, but can also apply to a geographic region like a city, country, state, etc. The term generally excludes the employers or management, and implies those involved in manual labour.
a. Pink-collar worker
b. Work-life balance
c. Division of labour
d. Workforce

9. In a military context, the _________ is the line of authority and responsibility along which orders are passed within a military unit and between different units. The term is also used in a civilian management context describing comparable hierarchical structures of authority.
a. 1990 Clean Air Act
b. 28-hour day
c. Chain of command
d. French leave

10. _________ is an organization's process of defining its strategy and making decisions on allocating its resources to pursue this strategy, including its capital and people. Various business analysis techniques can be used in _________, including SWOT analysis (Strengths, Weaknesses, Opportunities, and Threats) and PEST analysis (Political, Economic, Social, and Technological analysis) or STEER analysis involving Socio-cultural, Technological, Economic, Ecological, and Regulatory factors and EPISTEL (Environment, Political, Informatic, Social, Technological, Economic and Legal)

_________ is the formal consideration of an organization's future course. All _________ deals with at least one of three key questions:

1. 'What do we do?'
2. 'For whom do we do it?'
3. 'How do we excel?'

In business _________, the third question is better phrased 'How can we beat or avoid competition?'. (Bradford and Duncan, page 1.)

a. 1990 Clean Air Act
b. 28-hour day
c. 33 Strategies of War
d. Strategic planning

11. The _________ of an edge is $c_f(u,v) = c(u,v) - f(u,v)$. This defines a residual network denoted $G_f(V, E_f)$, giving the amount of available capacity. See that there can be an edge from u to v in the residual network, even though there is no edge from u to v in the original network.

a. 1990 Clean Air Act
b. Residual capacity
c. 33 Strategies of War
d. 28-hour day

12. A _________ is typically described as a deliberate plan of action to guide decisions and achieve rational outcome(s.) However, the term may also be used to denote what is actually done, even though it is unplanned.

The term may apply to government, private sector organizations and groups, and individuals.

a. 1990 Clean Air Act
b. Policy
c. 33 Strategies of War
d. 28-hour day

13. _________ refers to the structured transmission of data between organizations by electronic means. It is used to transfer electronic documents from one computer system to another (ie) from one trading partner to another trading partner. It is more than mere E-mail; for instance, organizations might replace bills of lading and even checks with appropriate _________ messages.

a. A4e
b. A Stake in the Outcome
c. Electronic data interchange
d. AAAI

14. An _________ is a private network that uses Internet protocols, network connectivity, and possibly the public telecommunication system to securely share part of an organization's information or operations with suppliers, vendors, partners, customers or other businesses. An _________ can be viewed as part of a company's intranet that is extended to users outside the company (e.g.: normally over the Internet.) It has also been described as a 'state of mind' in which the Internet is perceived as a way to do business with a preapproved set of other companies business-to-business (B2B), in isolation from all other Internet users.

a. AAAI
b. A Stake in the Outcome
c. Extranet
d. A4e

15. An _________ is a private computer network that uses Internet technologies to securely share any part of an organization's information or operational systems with its employees. Sometimes the term refers only to the organization's internal website, but often it is a more extensive part of the organization's computer infrastructure and private websites are an important component and focal point of internal communication and collaboration.

An _________ is built from the same concepts and technologies used for the Internet, such as client-server computing and the Internet Protocol Suite (TCP/IP.)

a. A4e
b. A Stake in the Outcome
c. AAAI
d. Intranet

16. _________ is a recursive process where two or more people or organizations work together in an intersection of common goals -- for example, an intellectual endeavor that is creative in nature--by sharing knowledge, learning and building consensus. _________ does not require leadership and can sometimes bring better results through decentralization and egalitarianism. In particular, teams that work collaboratively can obtain greater resources, recognition and reward when facing competition for finite resources._________ is also present in opposing goals exhibiting the notion of adversarial _________, though this is not a common case for using the term.

a. Collectivism
b. 28-hour day
c. 1990 Clean Air Act
d. Collaboration

17. _________ is the provision of service to customers before, during and after a purchase.

According to Turban et al. (2002), '_________ is a series of activities designed to enhance the level of customer satisfaction - that is, the feeling that a product or service has met the customer expectation.'

Its importance varies by product, industry and customer; defective or broken merchandise can be exchanged, often only with a receipt and within a specified time frame.

a. 1990 Clean Air Act
b. Service rate
c. 28-hour day
d. Customer service

18. _________ is an advertisement in which a particular product specifically mentions a competitor by name for the express purpose of showing why the competitor is inferior to the product naming it.

This should not be confused with parody advertisements, where a fictional product is being advertised for the purpose of poking fun at the particular advertisement, nor should it be confused with the use of a coined brand name for the purpose of comparing the product without actually naming an actual competitor. ('Wikipedia tastes better and is less filling than the Encyclopedia Galactica.')

In the 1980s, during what has been referred to as the cola wars, soft-drink manufacturer Pepsi ran a series of advertisements where people, caught on hidden camera, in a blind taste test, chose Pepsi over rival Coca-Cola.

a. 28-hour day
b. 33 Strategies of War
c. 1990 Clean Air Act
d. Comparative advertising

1. _________ refers to the stock of skills and knowledge embodied in the ability to perform labor so as to produce economic value. It is the skills and knowledge gained by a worker through education and experience. Many early economic theories refer to it simply as labor, one of three factors of production, and consider it to be a fungible resource -- homogeneous and easily interchangeable.

a. Deflation
b. Productivity management
c. Human Capital
d. Market structure

2. _________ is the strategic and coherent approach to the management of an organisation's most valued assets - the people working there who individually and collectively contribute to the achievement of the objectives of the business. The terms '_________' and 'human resources' (HR) have largely replaced the term 'personnel management' as a description of the processes involved in managing people in organizations. In simple sense, _________ means employing people, developing their resources, utilizing, maintaining and compensating their services in tune with the job and organizational requirement.

a. Job knowledge
b. Progressive discipline
c. Revolving door syndrome
d. Human resource management

3. _________ or _________ data refers to selected population characteristics as used in government, marketing or opinion research, or the _________ profiles used in such research. Note the distinction from the term 'demography' Commonly-used _________s include race, age, income, disabilities, mobility (in terms of travel time to work or number of vehicles available), educational attainment, home ownership, employment status, and even location.

a. Adam Smith
b. Affiliation
c. Abraham Harold Maslow
d. Demographic

4. The term '_________' refers to the concept of collecting information and attempting to spot a pattern in the information. In some fields of study, the term '_________' has more formally-defined meanings.

In project management _________ is a mathematical technique that uses historical results to predict future outcome.

a. Regression analysis
b. Least squares
c. Stepwise regression
d. Trend analysis

5. A _________ or labor union is an organization of workers who have banded together to achieve common goals in key areas and working conditions. The _________, through its leadership, bargains with the employer on behalf of union members (rank and file members) and negotiates labor contracts (Collective bargaining) with employers. This may include the negotiation of wages, work rules, complaint procedures, rules governing hiring, firing and promotion of workers, benefits, workplace safety and policies.
   a. Working time
   b. Trade union
   c. Company union
   d. Labour law

6. In organized labor, _________ is the method whereby workers organize together (usually in unions) to meet, converse, and negotiate upon the work conditions with their employers normally resulting in a written contract setting forth the wages, hours, and other conditions to be observed for a stipulated period.It is the practice in which union and company representatives meet to negotiate a new labor contract. In various national labor and employment law contexts, the term _________ takes on a more specific legal meaning. In a broad sense, however, it is the coming together of workers to negotiate their employment.
   a. Paid time off
   b. Labor rights
   c. Labour law
   d. Collective bargaining

7. _________ is a process of planning and controlling the performance or execution of any type of activity, such as:

- a project (project _________) or
- a process (process _________, sometimes referred to as the process performance measurement and management system.)

Organization's senior management is responsible for carrying out its _________.

   a. Work design
   b. Human Relations Movement
   c. Management process
   d. Participatory management

8. _________ comprises the actual output or results of an organization as measured against its intended outputs (or goals and objectives.)

Specialists in many fields are concerned with _________ including strategic planners, operations, finance, legal, and organizational development.

In recent years, many organizations have attempted to manage _________ using the balanced scorecard methodology where performance is tracked and measured in multiple dimensions such as:

- financial performance (e.g. shareholder return)
- customer service
- social responsibility (e.g. corporate citizenship, community outreach)
- employee stewardship

.

a. A Stake in the Outcome
b. AAAI
c. A4e
d. Organizational performance

9.

The terms _________ and positive action refer to policies that take race, ethnicity, or gender into consideration in an attempt to promote equal opportunity. The focus of such policies ranges from employment and education to public contracting and health programs. The impetus towards _________ is twofold: to maximize diversity in all levels of society, along with its presumed benefits, and to redress perceived disadvantages due to overt, institutional, or involuntary discrimination.

a. Affiliation
b. Affirmative action
c. Abraham Harold Maslow
d. Adam Smith

10. _________ is a civil designation for persons who are incorporated in a fixed or permanent way to a society or group: regular member of the working staff, permanent staff distinguished from a supernumerary.

The term '_________' and its counterpart, 'supernumerary,' originated in Spanish and Latin American academy and government; it is now also used in countries all over the world, such as France, the U.S., England, Italy, etc.

There are _________ members of surgical organizations, of universities, of gastronomical associations, etc.

a. Abraham Harold Maslow
b. Adam Smith
c. Affiliation
d. Numerary

11. _________ is an increasingly broadening term with which an organization, or other human system describes the combination of traditionally administrative personnel functions with acquisition and application of skills, knowledge and experience, Employee Relations and resource planning at various levels. The field draws upon concepts developed in Industrial/Organizational Psychology and System Theory. _________ has at least two related interpretations depending on context. The original usage derives from political economy and economics, where it was traditionally called labor, one of four factors of production although this perspective is changing as a function of new and ongoing research into more strategic approaches at national levels. This first usage is used more in terms of '_________ development', and can go beyond just organizations to the level of nations . The more traditional usage within corporations and businesses refers to the individuals within a firm or agency, and to the portion of the organization that deals with hiring, firing, training, and other personnel issues, typically referred to as `_________ management'.
a. Bradford Factor
b. Human resource management
c. Human resources
d. Progressive discipline

12. _________ refers to various methodologies for analyzing the requirements of a job.

The general purpose of _________ is to document the requirements of a job and the work performed. Job and task analysis is performed as a basis for later improvements, including: definition of a job domain; describing a job; developing performance appraisals, selection systems, promotion criteria, training needs assessment, and compensation plans.

a. Hersey-Blanchard situational theory
b. Work design
c. Job analysis
d. Management process

13. A _________ is a list of the general tasks and responsibilities of a position. Typically, it also includes to whom the position reports, specifications such as the qualifications needed by the person in the job, salary range for the position, etc. A _________ is usually developed by conducting a job analysis, which includes examining the tasks and sequences of tasks necessary to perform the job.

a. Recruitment advertising
b. Job description
c. Recruitment
d. Recruitment Process Insourcing

14. The _________ captures an expanded spectrum of values and criteria for measuring organizational success: economic, ecological and social. With the ratification of the United Nations and ICLEI _________ standard for urban and community accounting in early 2007, this became the dominant approach to public sector full cost accounting. Similar UN standards apply to natural capital and human capital measurement to assist in measurements required by _________, e.g. the ecoBudget standard for reporting ecological footprint.
a. 33 Strategies of War
b. 28-hour day
c. 1990 Clean Air Act
d. Triple bottom line

15. _________ refers to the process of screening, and selecting qualified people for a job at an organization or firm mid- and large-size organizations and companies often retain professional recruiters or outsource some of the process to _________ agencies. External _________ is the process of attracting and selecting employees from outside the organization.

The _________ industry has four main types of agencies: employment agencies, _________ websites and job search engines, 'headhunters' for executive and professional _________, and in-house _________.

a. Referral recruitment
b. Recruitment Process Outsourcing
c. Labour hire
d. Recruitment

16. The _________ is the labour pool in employment. It is generally used to describe those working for a single company or industry, but can also apply to a geographic region like a city, country, state, etc. The term generally excludes the employers or management, and implies those involved in manual labour.
a. Work-life balance
b. Workforce
c. Division of labour
d. Pink-collar worker

17. In game theory, an _________ is a set of moves or strategies taken by the players, or their payoffs resulting from the actions or strategies taken by all players. The two are complementary in that given knowledge of the set of strategies of all players, the final state of the game is known, as are any relevant payoffs. In a game where chance or a random event is involved, the _________ is not known from only the set of strategies, but is only realized when the random event(s) are realized.

a. AAAI
b. A Stake in the Outcome
c. A4e
d. Outcome

18. The term _________ in logic applies to arguments or statements.

An argument is valid if and only if the truth of its premises entails the truth of its conclusion, it would be self-contradictory to affirm the premises and deny the conclusion. The corresponding conditional of a valid argument is a logical truth and the negation of its corresponding conditional is a contradiction.

a. Simplification
b. 1990 Clean Air Act
c. Fuzzy logic
d. Validity

19. A chief executive officer (_________) or chief executive is one of the highest-ranking corporate officer (executive) or administrator in charge of total management. An individual selected as President and _________ of a corporation, company, organization, or agency, reports to the board of directors. In internal communication and press releases, many companies capitalize the term and those of other high positions, even when they are not proper nouns.

a. Portfolio manager
b. Chief executive officer
c. Director of communications
d. CEO

20. _________ is a forward looking process for setting goals and regularly checking progress toward achieving those goals. It is a continual feedback process whereby the actual outputs are measured and compared with the desired goals. Any discrepancy or gap is then fed back into changing the inputs of the process, so as to achieve the desired goals or outputs.

a. 28-hour day
b. 33 Strategies of War
c. 1990 Clean Air Act
d. Performance management

21. _________ is a method by which the job performance of an employee is evaluated _________ is a part of career development.

_________s are regular reviews of employee performance within organizations

Generally, the aims of a _________ are to:

- Give feedback on performance to employees.
- Identify employee training needs.
- Document criteria used to allocate organizational rewards.
- Form a basis for personnel decisions: salary increases, promotions, disciplinary actions, etc.
- Provide the opportunity for organizational diagnosis and development.
- Facilitate communication between employee and administraton
- Validate selection techniques and human resource policies to meet federal Equal Employment Opportunity requirements.

A common approach to assessing performance is to use a numerical or scalar rating system whereby managers are asked to score an individual against a number of objectives/attributes. In some companies, employees receive assessments from their manager, peers, subordinates and customers while also performing a self assessment.

a. Human resource management
b. Personnel management
c. Progressive discipline
d. Performance appraisal

22. In psychology research on behaviorism, _________ are scales used to report performance. _________ are normally presented vertically with scale points ranging from five to nine.

It is an appraisal method that aims to combine the benefits of narratives, critical incident incidents, and quantified ratings by anchoring a quantified scale with specific narrative examples of good or poor performance.

a. 28-hour day
b. Behaviorally anchored rating scales
c. 1990 Clean Air Act
d. 33 Strategies of War

23. _________ is a process of agreeing upon objectives within an organization so that management and employees agree to the objectives and understand what they are in the organization.

The term '_________' was first popularized by Peter Drucker in his 1954 book 'The Practice of Management'.

The essence of _________ is participative goal setting, choosing course of actions and decision making.

a. Business economics
b. Job enrichment
c. Clean sheet review
d. Management by objectives

24. A _________ is a set of categories designed to elicit information about a quantitative or a qualitative attribute. In the social sciences, common examples are the Likert scale and 1-10 _________s in which a person selects the number which is considered to reflect the perceived quality of a product.

A _________ is an instrument that requires the rater to assign the rated object that have numerals assigned to them.

a. Polytomous Rasch model
b. Thurstone scale
c. Spearman-Brown prediction formula
d. Rating scale

25. In human resources or industrial/organizational psychology, _________' 'multisource feedback,' or 'multisource assessment,' is feedback that comes from all around an employee. '360' refers to the 360 degrees in a circle, with an individual figuratively in the center of the circle. Feedback is provided by subordinates, peers, and supervisors.

a. Personnel management
b. Job knowledge
c. Revolving door syndrome
d. 360-degree feedback

26. _________ describes the situation when output from (or information about the result of) an event or phenomenon in the past will influence the same event/phenomenon in the present or future. When an event is part of a chain of cause-and-effect that forms a circuit or loop, then the event is said to 'feed back' into itself.

_________ is also a synonym for:

- _________ signal; the information about the initial event that is the basis for subsequent modification of the event.
- _________ loop; the causal path that leads from the initial generation of the _________ signal to the subsequent modification of the event.

_________ is a mechanism, process or signal that is looped back to control a system within itself. Such a loop is called a _________ loop.

a. Feedback loop
b. 1990 Clean Air Act
c. Positive feedback
d. Feedback

27. _________ is a term defined by the Oxford English Dictionary as an individual's 'course or progress through life '. It is usually considered to pertain to remunerative work (and sometimes also formal education.)

The etymology of the term is somewhat ironic in that it comes from the Latin word carrera, which means race .

a. Career planning
b. Nursing shortage
c. Spatial mismatch
d. Career

28. In organizational development (or OD), the study of _________ looks at:

- how individuals manage their careers within and between organizations
- and how organizations structure the career progress of their members, it can also be tied into succession planning within some organizations.

In personal development, _________ is:

- ' ... the total constellation of psychological, sociological, educational, physical, economic, and chance factors that combine to influence the nature and significance of work in the total lifespan of any given individual.'

- '... the lifelong psychological and behavioral processes as well as contextual influences shaping one's career over the life span. As such, _________ involves the person's creation of a career pattern, decision-making style, integration of life roles, values expression, and life-role self concepts.'

Figures in _________

- Jeff A. Brown
- Jesse B. Davis
- Caela Farren
- John L. Holland
- Kris Magnusson
- Frank Parsons
- Vance Peavy
- Edgar Schein
- Rino Schreuder
- Mark L. Savickas
- Donald Super

.

a. Horizontal integration
b. Career development
c. Sole proprietorship
d. Business process reengineering

29. The 'business case for _________', theorizes that in a global marketplace, a company that employs a diverse workforce (both men and women, people of many generations, people from ethnically and racially diverse backgrounds etc.) is better able to understand the demographics of the marketplace it serves and is thus better equipped to thrive in that marketplace than a company that has a more limited range of employee demographics.

An additional corollary suggests that a company that supports the _________ of its workforce can also improve employee satisfaction, productivity and retention.

a. Diversity
b. Trademark
c. Virtual team
d. Kanban

30. _________ is unwelcome harassment of a sexual nature, or based upon the receiving party's sex or gender. In some contexts or circumstances, _________ may be illegal. It includes a range of behavior from seemingly mild transgressions and annoyances to actual sexual abuse or sexual assault.

a. 28-hour day
b. Hypernorms
c. 1990 Clean Air Act
d. Sexual harassment

31. _________ is a contract between two parties, one being the employer and the other being the employee. An employee may be defined as: 'A person in the service of another under any contract of hire, express or implied, oral or written, where the employer has the power or right to control and direct the employee in the material details of how the work is to be performed.' Black's Law Dictionary page 471 (5th ed. 1979.)

a. Employment counsellor
b. Employment rate
c. Exit interview
d. Employment

32. _________ is a broad concept including proper prioritizing between career and ambition on one hand, compared with pleasure, leisure, family and spiritual development on the other.

As the separation between work and home life has diminished, this concept has become more relevant than ever before.

The expression was first used in the late 1970s to describe the balance between an individual's work and personal life.

a. Division of labour
b. Quality of working life
c. Work-life balance
d. Workforce

33. In general, a _________ is an arrangement to provide people with an income when they are no longer earning a regular income from employment.

The terms retirement plan or superannuation refer to a _________ granted upon retirement . Retirement plans may be set up by employers, insurance companies, the government or other institutions such as employer associations or trade unions.

a. State Compensation Insurance Fund

b. Wage

c. Pension insurance contract

d. Pension

1. The 'business case for _________', theorizes that in a global marketplace, a company that employs a diverse workforce (both men and women, people of many generations, people from ethnically and racially diverse backgrounds etc.) is better able to understand the demographics of the marketplace it serves and is thus better equipped to thrive in that marketplace than a company that has a more limited range of employee demographics.

An additional corollary suggests that a company that supports the _________ of its workforce can also improve employee satisfaction, productivity and retention.

a. Trademark
b. Virtual team
c. Kanban
d. Diversity

2. The _________ is the labour pool in employment. It is generally used to describe those working for a single company or industry, but can also apply to a geographic region like a city, country, state, etc. The term generally excludes the employers or management, and implies those involved in manual labour.
a. Work-life balance
b. Division of labour
c. Pink-collar worker
d. Workforce

3. The _________ captures an expanded spectrum of values and criteria for measuring organizational success: economic, ecological and social. With the ratification of the United Nations and ICLEI _________ standard for urban and community accounting in early 2007, this became the dominant approach to public sector full cost accounting. Similar UN standards apply to natural capital and human capital measurement to assist in measurements required by _________, e.g. the ecoBudget standard for reporting ecological footprint.
a. 33 Strategies of War
b. Triple bottom line
c. 1990 Clean Air Act
d. 28-hour day

4. _________ is the use of control systems (such as numerical control, programmable logic control, and other industrial control systems), in concert with other applications of information technology (such as computer-aided technologies [CAD, CAM, CAx]), to control industrial machinery and processes, reducing the need for human intervention. In the scope of industrialization, _________ is a step beyond mechanization. Whereas mechanization provided human operators with machinery to assist them with the physical requirements of work, _________ greatly reduces the need for human sensory and mental requirements as well.

a. A Stake in the Outcome
b. A4e
c. AAAI
d. Automation

5. As defined by Richard Beckhard, _________ is a planned, top-down, organization-wide effort to increase the organization's effectiveness and health. _________ is achieved through interventions in the organization's 'processes,' using behavioural science knowledge. According to Warren Bennis, _________ is a complex strategy intended to change the beliefs, attitudes, values, and structure of organizations so that they can better adapt to new technologies, markets, and challenges.
a. Organizational structure
b. Organizational culture
c. Organizational development
d. Informal organization

6. _________ is an idea in the field of Organizational studies and management which describes the psychology, attitudes, experiences, beliefs and Values (personal and cultural values) of an organization. It has been defined as 'the specific collection of values and norms that are shared by people and groups in an organization and that control the way they interact with each other and with stakeholders outside the organization.'

This definition continues to explain organizational values also known as 'beliefs and ideas about what kinds of goals members of an organization should pursue and ideas about the appropriate kinds or standards of behavior organizational members should use to achieve these goals. From organizational values develop organizational norms, guidelines or expectations that prescribe appropriate kinds of behavior by employees in particular situations and control the behavior of organizational members towards one another.'

_________ is not the same as corporate culture.

a. Organizational development
b. Organizational culture
c. Organizational effectiveness
d. Union shop

7. _________ is a civil designation for persons who are incorporated in a fixed or permanent way to a society or group: regular member of the working staff, permanent staff distinguished from a supernumerary.

The term '_________' and its counterpart, 'supernumerary,' originated in Spanish and Latin American academy and government; it is now also used in countries all over the world, such as France, the U.S., England, Italy, etc.

There are _________ members of surgical organizations, of universities, of gastronomical associations, etc.

a. Affiliation
b. Numerary
c. Adam Smith
d. Abraham Harold Maslow

8. In economics, _________ is the desire to own something and the ability to pay for it. The term _________ signifies the ability or the willingness to buy a particular commodity at a given point of time.
a. 28-hour day
b. Demand
c. 33 Strategies of War
d. 1990 Clean Air Act

9. _________ refers to a range of skills, tools, and techniques used to manage time when accomplishing specific tasks, projects and goals. This set encompass a wide scope of activities, and these include planning, allocating, setting goals, delegation, analysis of time spent, monitoring, organizing, scheduling, and prioritizing. Initially _________ referred to just business or work activities, but eventually the term broadened to include personal activities also.
a. Voice of the customer
b. Formula for Change
c. Cash cow
d. Time management

1. The _________ captures an expanded spectrum of values and criteria for measuring organizational success: economic, ecological and social. With the ratification of the United Nations and ICLEI _________ standard for urban and community accounting in early 2007, this became the dominant approach to public sector full cost accounting. Similar UN standards apply to natural capital and human capital measurement to assist in measurements required by _________, e.g. the ecoBudget standard for reporting ecological footprint.

a. 33 Strategies of War
b. 1990 Clean Air Act
c. 28-hour day
d. Triple bottom line

2. _________ describes how content an individual is with his or her job.

The happier people are within their job, the more satisfied they are said to be. _________ is not the same as motivation, although it is clearly linked.

a. Human relations
b. Goal-setting theory
c. Job analysis
d. Job satisfaction

3. _________ are a special type of work behavior that are defined as individual behaviors that are beneficial to the organization and are discretionary, not directly or explicitly recognized by the formal reward system. These behaviors are rather a matter of personal choice, such that their omission are not generally understood as punishable. _________ are thought to have an important impact on the effectiveness and efficiency of work teams and organizations, therefore contributing to the overall productivity of the organization.

a. AAAI
b. A4e
c. A Stake in the Outcome
d. Organizational citizenship behaviors

4. In a human resources context, _________ or labor _________ is the rate at which an employer gains and loses employees. Simple ways to describe it are 'how long employees tend to stay' or 'the rate of traffic through the revolving door.' _________ is measured for individual companies and for their industry as a whole. If an employer is said to have a high _________ relative to its competitors, it means that employees of that company have a shorter average tenure than those of other companies in the same industry.

a. Continuous
b. Career portfolios
c. Ten year occupational employment projection
d. Turnover

5. _________ refers to metrics and measures of output from production processes, per unit of input. Labor _________, for example, is typically measured as a ratio of output per labor-hour, an input. _________ may be conceived of as a metrics of the technical or engineering efficiency of production.

a. Master production schedule
b. Value engineering
c. Remanufacturing
d. Productivity

6. _________ is a habitual pattern of absence from a duty or obligation.

Frequent absence from the workplace may be indicative of poor morale or of sick building syndrome. However, many employers have implemented absence policies which make no distinction between absences for genuine illness and absence for inappropriate reasons.

a. Absenteeism
b. A4e
c. Emanation of the state
d. A Stake in the Outcome

7. _________ is an advertisement in which a particular product specifically mentions a competitor by name for the express purpose of showing why the competitor is inferior to the product naming it.

This should not be confused with parody advertisements, where a fictional product is being advertised for the purpose of poking fun at the particular advertisement, nor should it be confused with the use of a coined brand name for the purpose of comparing the product without actually naming an actual competitor. ('Wikipedia tastes better and is less filling than the Encyclopedia Galactica.')

In the 1980s, during what has been referred to as the cola wars, soft-drink manufacturer Pepsi ran a series of advertisements where people, caught on hidden camera, in a blind taste test, chose Pepsi over rival Coca-Cola.

a. Comparative advertising
b. 1990 Clean Air Act
c. 28-hour day
d. 33 Strategies of War

8. _________, a business term, is a measure of how products and services supplied by a company meet or surpass customer expectation. It is seen as a key performance indicator within business and is part of the four perspectives of a Balanced Scorecard.

In a competitive marketplace where businesses compete for customers, _________ is seen as a key differentiator and increasingly has become a key element of business strategy.

a. Customer satisfaction
b. Critical Success Factor
c. Horizontal integration
d. Foreign ownership

9.

_________ is a commonly used, yet poorly defined concept in industrial and organizational psychology, the branch of psychology that deals with the workplace. It most commonly refers to whether a person performs their job well. Despite the confusion over how it should be exactly defined, performance is an extremely important criterion that relates to organizational outcomes and success.

a. Job performance
b. 33 Strategies of War
c. 1990 Clean Air Act
d. 28-hour day

10. As defined by Richard Beckhard, _________ is a planned, top-down, organization-wide effort to increase the organization's effectiveness and health. _________ is achieved through interventions in the organization's 'processes,' using behavioural science knowledge. According to Warren Bennis, _________ is a complex strategy intended to change the beliefs, attitudes, values, and structure of organizations so that they can better adapt to new technologies, markets, and challenges.

a. Organizational structure
b. Organizational culture
c. Informal organization
d. Organizational development

11. _________ is an uncomfortable feeling caused by holding two contradictory ideas simultaneously. The 'ideas' or 'cognitions' in question may include attitudes and beliefs, and also the awareness of one's behavior. The theory of _________ proposes that people have a motivational drive to reduce dissonance by changing their attitudes, beliefs, and behaviors, or by justifying or rationalizing their attitudes, beliefs, and behaviors.

a. Cognitive bias
b. Quantitative psychology
c. Trait theory
d. Cognitive dissonance

12. _________ is a term in psychology which refers to a person's belief about what causes the good or bad results in his or her life, either in general or in a specific area such as health or academics. Understanding of the concept was developed by Julian B. Rotter in 1954, and has since become an important aspect of personality studies.

_________ refers to the extent to which individuals believe that they can control events that affect them.

a. Self-enhancement
b. Social loafing
c. Machiavellianism
d. Locus of control

13. _________ is, according to the OED, 'the employment of cunning and duplicity in statecraft or in general conduct', deriving from the Italian Renaissance diplomat and writer Niccolò Machiavelli, who wrote Il Principe and other works. Machiavellian and variants became very popular in the late 16th century in English, though '_________' itself is first cited by the OED from 1626. The word has a similar use in modern psychology.
a. Personal space
b. Self-enhancement
c. Machiavellianism
d. Persuasion

14. In psychology, _________ reflects a person's overall evaluation or appraisal of his or her own worth.

_________ encompasses beliefs (for example, 'I am competent/incompetent') and emotions (for example, triumph/despair, pride/shame.) Behavior may reflect _________

a. Self-esteem
b. 28-hour day
c. 33 Strategies of War
d. 1990 Clean Air Act

15. _________ is one of the managerial functions like planning, organizing, staffing and directing. It is an important function because it helps to check the errors and to take the corrective action so that deviation from standards are minimized and stated goals of the organization are achieved in desired manner.According to modern concepts, _________ is a foreseeing action whereas earlier concept of _________ was used only when errors were detected. _________ in management means setting standards, measuring actual performance and taking corrective action.

a. Schedule of reinforcement
b. Turnover
c. Decision tree pruning
d. Control

16. In statistics, _________ is:

- the arithmetic _________
- the expected value of a random variable, which is also called the population _________.

It is sometimes stated that the '_________' _________s average. This is incorrect if '_________' is taken in the specific sense of 'arithmetic _________' as there are different types of averages: the _________, median, and mode. Other simple statistical analyses use measures of spread, such as range, interquartile range, or standard deviation. For a real-valued random variable X, the _________ is the expectation of X. Note that not every probability distribution has a defined _________; see the Cauchy distribution for an example.

a. Control chart
b. Statistical inference
c. Correlation
d. Mean

17. In sociology and social psychology, _________ is the process through which people try to control the impressions other people form of them. It is a goal-directed conscious or unconscious attempt to influence the perceptions of other people about a person, object or event by regulating and controlling information in social interaction. It is usually used synonymously with self-presentation, if a person tries to influence the perception of their image.

a. Impression management
b. A4e
c. A Stake in the Outcome
d. AAAI

18. In decision theory and estimation theory, the _________ of an estimator, $\hat{\theta}$, of an unknown parameter of the distribution, θ, is the expected value of the loss function

$$R(\theta, \hat{\theta}) = \mathbb{E}_\theta L(\theta, \hat{\theta}) = \int L(\theta, \hat{\theta})\, dP_\theta.$$

where dP_θ is a probability measure parametrized by θ.

- For a scalar parameter θ and a quadratic loss function,

  $$L(\theta, \hat{\theta}) = (\theta - \hat{\theta})^2$$

  the _________ function becomes the mean squared error of the estimate,

  $$R(\theta, \hat{\theta}) = E_\theta(\theta - \hat{\theta})^2$$

- In density estimation, the unknown parameter is probability density itself. The loss function is typically chosen to be a norm in an appropriate function space. For example, for L^2 norm,

  $$L(f, \hat{f}) = \|f - \hat{f}\|_2^2$$

  the _________ function becomes the mean integrated squared error

  $$R(f, \hat{f}) = E\|f - \hat{f}\|^2$$

.

a. Financial modeling
b. Risk aversion
c. Linear model
d. Risk

19. _________ , often measured as an _________ Quotient (EQ), is a term that describes the ability, capacity, skill or (in the case of the trait _________ model) a self-perceived ability, to identify, assess, and manage the emotions of one's self, of others, and of groups. Different models have been proposed for the definition of _________ and disagreement exists as to how the term should be used. Despite these disagreements, which are often highly technical, the ability _________ and trait _________ models (but not the mixed models) are enjoying considerable support in the literature and have successful applications in many different domains.

a. A Stake in the Outcome
b. AAAI
c. Emotional intelligence
d. A4e

20. _________ is a social psychology theory developed by Fritz Heider, Harold Kelley, Edward E. Jones, and Lee Ross.

The theory is concerned with the ways in which people explain (or attribute) the behavior of others or themselves (self-attribution) with something else. It explores how individuals 'attribute' causes to events and how this cognitive perception effects their usefulness in an organization.

a. A Stake in the Outcome
b. A4e
c. Attribution theory
d. AAAI

21. In attribution theory, the _________ is a theory describing cognitive tendency to predominantly over-value dispositional explanations for the observed behaviors of others, thus under-valuing or acknowledging the potentiality of situational attributions or situational explanations for the behavioral motives of others. In other words, people predominantly presume that the actions of others are indicative of the 'kind' of person they are, rather than the kind of situations that compels their behavior. However, the over attribution effect generally does not account for our own ability to self-justify our behaviors; we tend to prefer interpreting our own actions in terms of the situational variables accessible to our awareness.

a. Confirmation bias
b. Pygmalion effect
c. Halo effect
d. Fundamental attribution error

22. The _________ refers to a cognitive bias whereby the perception of a particular trait is influenced by the perception of the former traits in a sequence of interpretations.

Edward L. Thorndike was the first to support the _________ with empirical research. In a psychology study published in 1920, Thorndike asked commanding officers to rate their soldiers; Thorndike found high cross-correlation between all positive and all negative traits.

a. Sunk costs
b. Distinction bias
c. Cognitive biases
d. Halo effect

23. A _________ occurs when people attribute their successes to internal or personal factors but attribute their failures to situational factors beyond their control. The _________ can be seen in the common human tendency to take credit for success but to deny responsibility for failure. It may also manifest itself as a tendency for people to evaluate ambiguous information in a way that is beneficial to their interests.

a. Fundamental attribution error
b. Pygmalion effect
c. Halo effect
d. Self-serving bias

24. _________ is the use of consequences to modify the occurrence and form of behavior. _________ is distinguished from classical conditioning (also called respondent conditioning, or Pavlovian conditioning) in that _________ deals with the modification of 'voluntary behavior' or operant behavior. Operant behavior 'operates' on the environment and is maintained by its consequences, while classical conditioning deals with the conditioning of respondent behaviors which are elicited by antecedent conditions.

a. Outsourcing
b. Unemployment insurance
c. Occupational Safety and Health Administration
d. Operant conditioning

25. _________ refers to training in different ways to improve overall performance. It takes advantage of the particular effectiveness of each training method, while at the same time attempting to neglect the shortcomings of that method by combining it with other methods that address its weaknesses.

Cross training is employee-employer field means, training employees to do one another's work.

a. 33 Strategies of War
b. 28-hour day
c. 1990 Clean Air Act
d. Cross-training

26. In operant conditioning, _________ occurs when an event following a response causes an increase in the probability of that response occurring in the future. Response strength can be assessed by measures such as the frequency with which the response is made (for example, a pigeon may peck a key more times in the session), or the speed with which it is made (for example, a rat may run a maze faster.) The environment change contingent upon the response is called a reinforcer.

a. Diminishing Manufacturing Sources and Material Shortages
b. Historiometry
c. Meetings, Incentives, Conferences, and Exhibitions
d. Reinforcement

27. _________ is the theory that people learn new behavior through overt reinforcement or punishment, or via observational learning of the social actors in their environment. If people observe positive, desired outcomes in the observed behavior, they are more likely to model, imitate, and adopt the behavior themselves.

_________ is derived from the work of Gabriel Tarde (1843-1904) which proposed that social learning occurred through four main stages of limitation:

- close contact,
- imitation of superiors,
- understanding of concepts,
- role model behaviour

It consists of 3 parts observing, imitating, and reinforcements

Julian Rotter moved away from theories based on psychosis and behaviourism, and developed a learning theory. In Social Learning and Clinical Psychology (1954), Rotter suggests that the effect of behaviour has an impact on the motivation of people to engage in that specific behaviour.

a. 28-hour day
b. 33 Strategies of War
c. Social learning theory
d. 1990 Clean Air Act

28. _________ is a term used to describe the demographic cohort following Generation X. Its members are often referred to as 'Millennials' or 'Echo Boomers') . There are no precise dates for when Gen Y begins and ends. Most commentators use dates from the early 1980s to early 1990s.

a. Generation Y
b. Giovanni Agnelli
c. David Wittig
d. Benjamin R. Barber

1. The goal of most research on _________ is to learn why and how small groups change over time. To do this, researchers examine patterns of change and continuity in groups over time. Aspects of a group that might be studied include the quality of the output produced by a group, the type and frequency of its activities, its cohesiveness, the existence of conflict, etc.

a. Group development
b. 1990 Clean Air Act
c. 28-hour day
d. 33 Strategies of War

2. _________ has been described as the 'process of social influence in which one person can enlist the aid and support of others in the accomplishment of a common task' . A definition more inclusive of followers comes from Alan Keith of Genentech who said '_________ is ultimately about creating a way for people to contribute to making something extraordinary happen.'

_________ is one of the most salient aspects of the organizational context. However, defining _________ has been challenging.

a. 28-hour day
b. Leadership
c. Situational leadership
d. 1990 Clean Air Act

3. The _________ captures an expanded spectrum of values and criteria for measuring organizational success: economic, ecological and social. With the ratification of the United Nations and ICLEI _________ standard for urban and community accounting in early 2007, this became the dominant approach to public sector full cost accounting. Similar UN standards apply to natural capital and human capital measurement to assist in measurements required by _________, e.g. the ecoBudget standard for reporting ecological footprint.

a. Triple bottom line
b. 1990 Clean Air Act
c. 33 Strategies of War
d. 28-hour day

4. _________ is a civil designation for persons who are incorporated in a fixed or permanent way to a society or group: regular member of the working staff, permanent staff distinguished from a supernumerary.

The term '_________' and its counterpart, 'supernumerary,' originated in Spanish and Latin American academy and government; it is now also used in countries all over the world, such as France, the U.S., England, Italy, etc.

There are _________ members of surgical organizations, of universities, of gastronomical associations, etc.

a. Adam Smith
b. Affiliation
c. Abraham Harold Maslow
d. Numerary

5. The 'business case for _________', theorizes that in a global marketplace, a company that employs a diverse workforce (both men and women, people of many generations, people from ethnically and racially diverse backgrounds etc.) is better able to understand the demographics of the marketplace it serves and is thus better equipped to thrive in that marketplace than a company that has a more limited range of employee demographics.

An additional corollary suggests that a company that supports the _________ of its workforce can also improve employee satisfaction, productivity and retention.

a. Virtual team
b. Trademark
c. Kanban
d. Diversity

6. The _________ is the labour pool in employment. It is generally used to describe those working for a single company or industry, but can also apply to a geographic region like a city, country, state, etc. The term generally excludes the employers or management, and implies those involved in manual labour.
a. Pink-collar worker
b. Work-life balance
c. Division of labour
d. Workforce

7. '_________ is a conflict among the roles corresponding to two or more statuses.'

_________ is a special form of social conflict that takes place when one is forced to take on two different and incompatible roles at the same time. Consider the example of a doctor who is himself a patient, or who must decide whether he should be present for his daughter's birthday party (in his role as 'father') or attend an ailing patient (as 'doctor'.) (Also compare the psychological concept of cognitive dissonance.)

a. Soft skill
b. Social network analysis
c. Role conflict
d. Self-disclosure

8. _________ is a type of thought exhibited by group members who try to minimize conflict and reach consensus without critically testing, analyzing, and evaluating ideas. Individual creativity, uniqueness, and independent thinking are lost in the pursuit of group cohesiveness, as are the advantages of reasonable balance in choice and thought that might normally be obtained by making decisions as a group. During _________, members of the group avoid promoting viewpoints outside the comfort zone of consensus thinking.

a. Psychological statistics
b. Self-report inventory
c. Diffusion of responsibility
d. Groupthink

9. In the social psychology of groups, _________ is the phenomenon of people making less effort to achieve a goal when they work in a group than when they work alone. This is seen as one of the main reasons groups are sometimes less productive than the combined performance of their members working as individuals.

- Ringelmann, Max : 1913

Research began in 1913 with Max Ringelmann's study. He found that when he asked a group of men to pull on a rope, that they did not pull as hard, or put as much effort into the activity, as they did when they were pulling alone.

a. Social loafing
b. Machiavellianism
c. Personal space
d. Self-enhancement

10. _________ refers to the long-term management of intractable conflicts. It is the label for the variety of ways by which people handle grievances--standing up for what they consider to be right and against what they consider to be wrong. Those ways include such diverse phenomena as gossip, ridicule, lynching, terrorism, warfare, feuding, genocide, law, mediation, and avoidance.

a. 1990 Clean Air Act
b. Conflict Management
c. 28-hour day
d. 33 Strategies of War

11. _________ Movement refers to those researchers of organizational development who study the behavior of people in groups, in particular workplace groups. It originated in the 1920s' Hawthorne studies, which examined the effects of social relations, motivation and employee satisfaction on factory productivity. The movement viewed workers in terms of their psychology and fit with companies, rather than as interchangeable parts.

a. Hersey-Blanchard situational theory
b. Participatory management
c. Work design
d. Human relations

12. In game theory, an _________ is a set of moves or strategies taken by the players, or their payoffs resulting from the actions or strategies taken by all players. The two are complementary in that given knowledge of the set of strategies of all players, the final state of the game is known, as are any relevant payoffs. In a game where chance or a random event is involved, the _________ is not known from only the set of strategies, but is only realized when the random event(s) are realized.
a. A Stake in the Outcome
b. A4e
c. AAAI
d. Outcome

13. _________ is a concept in ethics with several meanings. It is often used synonymously with such concepts as responsibility, answerability, enforcement, blameworthiness, liability and other terms associated with the expectation of account-giving. As an aspect of governance, it has been central to discussions related to problems in both the public and private (corporation) worlds.
a. Usury
b. A4e
c. Accountability
d. A Stake in the Outcome

14. _________ is the term used to describe a situation where different entities cooperate advantageously for a final outcome. Simply defined, it means that the whole is greater than the sum of the individual parts. Although the whole will be greater than each individual part, this is not the concept of _________.
a. Synergy
b. 28-hour day
c. 33 Strategies of War
d. 1990 Clean Air Act

15. A _________ is a group of employees from various functional areas of the organization - research, engineering, marketing, finance. human resources, and operations, for example - who are all focused on a specific objective and are responsible to work as a team to improve coordination and innovation across divisions and resolve mutual problems.

a. Sociotechnical systems
b. Cross-functional team
c. Graduate recruitment
d. Goal-setting theory

16. A _________ -- also known as a geographically dispersed team -- is a group of individuals who work across time, space, and organizational boundaries with links strengthened by webs of communication technology. They have complementary skills and are committed to a common purpose, have interdependent performance goals, and share an approach to work for which they hold themselves mutually accountable. Geographically dispersed teams allow organizations to hire and retain the best people regardless of location.
a. Trademark
b. Risk management
c. Kanban
d. Virtual team

17. A chief executive officer (_________) or chief executive is one of the highest-ranking corporate officer (executive) or administrator in charge of total management. An individual selected as President and _________ of a corporation, company, organization, or agency, reports to the board of directors. In internal communication and press releases, many companies capitalize the term and those of other high positions, even when they are not proper nouns.
a. CEO
b. Director of communications
c. Portfolio manager
d. Chief executive officer

1. Maslow's _________ is a theory in psychology, proposed by Abraham Maslow in his 1943 paper A Theory of Human Motivation, which he subsequently extended to include his observations of humans' innate curiosity.

Maslow's _________ is predetermined in order of importance. It is often depicted as a pyramid consisting of five levels: the lowest level is associated with physiological needs, while the uppermost level is associated with self-actualization needs, particularly those related to identity and purpose. Deficiency needs must be met first. Once these are met, seeking to satisfy growth needs drives personal growth. The higher needs in this hierarchy only come into focus when the lower needs in the pyramid are met.

a. 33 Strategies of War
b. 1990 Clean Air Act
c. Hierarchy of needs
d. 28-hour day

2. _________ is a term that has been used in various psychology theories, often in slightly different ways (e.g., Goldstein, Maslow, Rogers.) The term was originally introduced by the organismic theorist Kurt Goldstein for the motive to realise all of one's potentialities. In his view, it is the master motive--indeed, the only real motive a person has, all others being merely manifestations of it.

a. 33 Strategies of War
b. Self-actualization
c. 1990 Clean Air Act
d. 28-hour day

3. _________ and Theory Y are theories of human motivation created and developed by Douglas McGregor at the MIT Sloan School of Management in the 1960s that have been used in human resource management, organizational behavior, organizational communication and organizational development. They describe two very different attitudes toward workforce motivation. McGregor felt that companies followed either one or the other approach.

In _________, which many managers practice, management assumes employees are inherently lazy and will avoid work if they can. They inherently dislike work. Because of this, workers need to be closely supervised and comprehensive systems of controls developed.

a. Job enrichment
b. Cash cow
c. Management team
d. Theory X

4. Theory X and _________ are theories of human motivation created and developed by Douglas McGregor at the MIT Sloan School of Management in the 1960s that have been used in human resource management, organizational behavior, organizational communication and organizational development. They describe two very different attitudes toward workforce motivation. McGregor felt that companies followed either one or the other approach.

In _________, management assumes employees may be ambitious and self-motivated and exercise self-control. It is believed that employees enjoy their mental and physical work duties.

a. Design leadership
b. Contingency theory
c. Business Workflow Analysis
d. Theory Y

5. _________ are job factors that can cause dissatisfaction if missing but do not necessarily motivate employees if increased.

_________ have mostly to do with the job environment. These factors are important or notable only when they are lacking.

a. Split shift
b. Work system
c. Work-at-home scheme
d. Hygiene factors

6. _________ was developed by Frederick Herzberg, a psychologist who found that job satisfaction and job dissatisfaction acted independently of each other. _________ states that there are certain factors in the workplace that cause job satisfaction, while a separate set of factors cause dissatisfaction.

a. Need for power
b. Two-factor theory
c. Need for Achievement
d. 1990 Clean Air Act

7. _________ describes how content an individual is with his or her job.

The happier people are within their job, the more satisfied they are said to be. _________ is not the same as motivation, although it is clearly linked.

a. Human relations
b. Job analysis
c. Goal-setting theory
d. Job satisfaction

8. _________ has become one of the most popular theories in organizational psychology.

Goal setting has been a formula used for acheivement since the early 1800s. The form and pattern has cahanged drastically over the years and there is still much debate as to what is the most efective pattern to follow.

a. Corporate Culture
b. Human relations
c. Goal-setting theory
d. Job satisfaction

9. _________ refers to an individual's desire for significant accomplishment, mastering of skills, control, or high standards. The term was introduced by the psychologist, David McClelland.

_________ is related to the difficulty of tasks people choose to undertake.

a. Two-factor theory
b. Need for power
c. 1990 Clean Air Act
d. Need for achievement

10. The _________ is a term that was popularised by David McClelland and describes a person's need to feel a sense of involvement and 'belonging' within a social group. However, it should be recognised that McClellend's thinking was strongly influenced by the pioneering work of Henry Murray who first identified underlying psychological human needs and motivational processes (1938.) It was Murray who set out a taxonomy of needs, including Achievement, Power and Affiliation - and placed these in the context of an integrated motivational model.

a. Polynomial conjoint measurement
b. Need for affiliation
c. SESAMO
d. Strong-Campbell Interest Inventory

11. _________ is a term that was popularized by renowned psychologist David McClelland in 1961. However, it should be recognized that McClellend's thinking was strongly influenced by the pioneering work of Henry Murray who first identified underlying psychological human needs and motivational processes (1938.) It was Murray who set out a taxonomy of needs, including Achievement, Power and Affiliation - and placed these in the context of an integrated motivational model.

a. 1990 Clean Air Act
b. Two-factor theory
c. Need for power
d. Need for Achievement

12. In law, _________ is the term to describe a partnership between two or more parties.

In England a number of statutes on the subject have been passed, the chief being the Bastardy Act of 1845, and the Bastardy Laws Amendment Acts of 1872 and 1873. The mother of a bastard may summon the putative father to petty sessions within twelve months of the birth (or at any later time if he is proved to have contributed to the child's support within twelve months after the birth), and the justices, as after hearing evidence on both sides, may, if the mother's evidence be corroborated in some material particular, adjudge the man to be the putative father of the child, and order him to pay a sum not exceeding five shillings a week for its maintenance, together with a sum for expenses incidental to the birth, or the funeral expenses, if it has died before the date of order, and the costs of the proceedings.

a. Affiliation
b. Affiliation
c. Adam Smith
d. Abraham Harold Maslow

13. _________ is the belief that one is capable of performing in a certain manner to attain certain goals. It is a belief that one has the capabilities to execute the courses of actions required to manage prospective situations. Unlike efficacy, which is the power to produce an effect (in essence, competence), _________ is the belief (whether or not accurate) that one has the power to produce that effect.

a. 33 Strategies of War
b. 1990 Clean Air Act
c. 28-hour day
d. Self-efficacy

14. In operant conditioning, _________ occurs when an event following a response causes an increase in the probability of that response occurring in the future. Response strength can be assessed by measures such as the frequency with which the response is made (for example, a pigeon may peck a key more times in the session), or the speed with which it is made (for example, a rat may run a maze faster.) The environment change contingent upon the response is called a reinforcer.

a. Diminishing Manufacturing Sources and Material Shortages
b. Meetings, Incentives, Conferences, and Exhibitions
c. Historiometry
d. Reinforcement

15. _________ is a way of expressing knowledge or belief that an event will occur or has occurred. In mathematics the concept has been given an exact meaning in _________ theory, that is used extensively in such areas of study as mathematics, statistics, finance, gambling, science, and philosophy to draw conclusions about the likelihood of potential events and the underlying mechanics of complex systems.

The word _________ does not have a consistent direct definition.

a. Standard deviation
b. Probability
c. Time series analysis
d. Statistics

16. In organizational development (OD), _________ is the application of Socio-Technical Systems principles and techniques to the humanization of work.

The aims of _________ to improved job satisfaction, to improved through-put, to improved quality and to reduced employee problems, e.g., grievances, absenteeism.

Under scientific management people would be directed by reason and the problems of industrial unrest would be appropriately (i.e., scientifically) addressed.

a. Graduate recruitment
b. Path-goal theory
c. Work design
d. Management process

17. _________ means increasing the scope of a job through extending the range of its job duties and responsibilities. This contradicts the principles of specialisation and the division of labour whereby work is divided into small units, each of which is performed repetitively by an individual worker. Some motivational theories suggest that the boredom and alienation caused by the division of labour can actually cause efficiency to fall.
a. Job enlargement
b. Mock interview
c. Delayering
d. Centralization

18. _________ is an attempt to motivate employees by giving them the opportunity to use the range of their abilities. It is an idea that was developed by the American psychologist Frederick Herzberg in the 1950s. It can be contrasted to job enlargement which simply increases the number of tasks without changing the challenge.
a. Catfish effect
b. C-A-K-E
c. Cash cow
d. Job enrichment

19. _________ is one of the managerial functions like planning, organizing, staffing and directing. It is an important function because it helps to check the errors and to take the corrective action so that deviation from standards are minimized and stated goals of the organization are achieved in desired manner.According to modern concepts, _________ is a foreseeing action whereas earlier concept of _________ was used only when errors were detected. _________ in management means setting standards, measuring actual performance and taking corrective action.

a. Control
b. Turnover
c. Schedule of reinforcement
d. Decision tree pruning

20. In game theory, an _________ is a set of moves or strategies taken by the players, or their payoffs resulting from the actions or strategies taken by all players. The two are complementary in that given knowledge of the set of strategies of all players, the final state of the game is known, as are any relevant payoffs. In a game where chance or a random event is involved, the _________ is not known from only the set of strategies, but is only realized when the random event(s) are realized.

a. Outcome
b. A Stake in the Outcome
c. AAAI
d. A4e

21. _________ describes the situation when output from (or information about the result of) an event or phenomenon in the past will influence the same event/phenomenon in the present or future. When an event is part of a chain of cause-and-effect that forms a circuit or loop, then the event is said to 'feed back' into itself.

_________ is also a synonym for:

- _________ signal; the information about the initial event that is the basis for subsequent modification of the event.
- _________ loop; the causal path that leads from the initial generation of the _________ signal to the subsequent modification of the event.

_________ is a mechanism, process or signal that is looped back to control a system within itself. Such a loop is called a _________ loop.

a. Feedback
b. Positive feedback
c. Feedback loop
d. 1990 Clean Air Act

22. _________ is the self-government of a nation, country or some portion thereof, generally exercising sovereignty.

The term _________ is used in contrast to subjugation, which refers to a region as a 'territory' --subject to the political and military control of an external government. The word is sometimes used in a weaker sense to contrast with hegemony, the indirect control of one nation by another, more powerful nation.

a. A4e
b. A Stake in the Outcome
c. AAAI
d. Independence

23. A _________ is a list of the general tasks and responsibilities of a position. Typically, it also includes to whom the position reports, specifications such as the qualifications needed by the person in the job, salary range for the position, etc. A _________ is usually developed by conducting a job analysis, which includes examining the tasks and sequences of tasks necessary to perform the job.
a. Recruitment Process Insourcing
b. Recruitment
c. Recruitment advertising
d. Job description

24. The _________ captures an expanded spectrum of values and criteria for measuring organizational success: economic, ecological and social. With the ratification of the United Nations and ICLEI _________ standard for urban and community accounting in early 2007, this became the dominant approach to public sector full cost accounting. Similar UN standards apply to natural capital and human capital measurement to assist in measurements required by _________, e.g. the ecoBudget standard for reporting ecological footprint.
a. 1990 Clean Air Act
b. 33 Strategies of War
c. 28-hour day
d. Triple bottom line

25. _________ attempts to explain relational satisfaction in terms of perceptions of fair/unfair distributions of resources within interpersonal relationships. _________ is considered as one of the justice theories, It was first developed in 1962 by John Stacey Adams, a workplace and behavioral psychologist, who asserted that employees seek to maintain equity between the inputs that they bring to a job and the outcomes that they receive from it against the perceived inputs and outcomes of others (Adams, 1965.) The belief is that people value fair treatment which causes them to be motivated to keep the fairness maintained within the relationships of their co-workers and the organization.

a. AAAI
b. A Stake in the Outcome
c. Equity theory
d. A4e

26. _________ is about the mental processes regarding choice, or choosing. It explains the processes that an individual undergoes to make choices. In organizational behavior study, _________ is a motivation theory first proposed by Victor Vroom of the Yale School of Management.
a. A Stake in the Outcome
b. AAAI
c. A4e
d. Expectancy theory

27. _________ is one of the four elements of marketing mix. An organization or set of organizations (go-betweens) involved in the process of making a product or service available for use or consumption by a consumer or business user.

The other three parts of the marketing mix are product, pricing, and promotion.

a. Missing completely at random
b. Matching theory
c. Job creation programs
d. Distribution

28. _________, e-commuting, e-work, telework, working from home (WFH), or working at home (WAH) is a work arrangement in which employees enjoy flexibility in working location and hours. In other words, the daily commute to a central place of work is replaced by telecommunication links. Many work from home, while others, occasionally also referred to as nomad workers or web commuters utilize mobile telecommunications technology to work from coffee shops or myriad other locations.
a. 1990 Clean Air Act
b. 28-hour day
c. 33 Strategies of War
d. Telecommuting

29. The 'business case for _________', theorizes that in a global marketplace, a company that employs a diverse workforce (both men and women, people of many generations, people from ethnically and racially diverse backgrounds etc.) is better able to understand the demographics of the marketplace it serves and is thus better equipped to thrive in that marketplace than a company that has a more limited range of employee demographics.

An additional corollary suggests that a company that supports the _________ of its workforce can also improve employee satisfaction, productivity and retention.

a. Diversity
b. Kanban
c. Trademark
d. Virtual team

30. The _________ is the labour pool in employment. It is generally used to describe those working for a single company or industry, but can also apply to a geographic region like a city, country, state, etc. The term generally excludes the employers or management, and implies those involved in manual labour.
a. Division of labour
b. Pink-collar worker
c. Work-life balance
d. Workforce

31. The legal _________ varies from nation to nation. The weekend is a part of the week usually lasting one or two days in which most paid workers do not work.

In Muslim-majority countries the legal work week in the Middle East is typically either Saturday through Wednesday , Saturday through Thursday or Sunday through Thursday as in Egypt.

a. Day One Christian Ministries
b. Business day
c. Workweek
d. Working Time Directive

32. _________ is a management technique pioneered by Michael Phillips in San Francisco in the late '60's and early '70s. The concept's most visible success was by Jack Stack and his team at SRC Holdings and popularized in 1995 by John Case. The technique is to give employees all relevant financial information about the company so they can make better decisions as workers.
a. AAAI
b. Open-book management
c. A4e
d. A Stake in the Outcome

33. _________ are formal records of the financial activities of a business, person, or other entity. In British English, including United Kingdom company law, _________ are often referred to as accounts, although the term _________ is also used, particularly by accountants.

_________ provide an overview of a business or person's financial condition in both short and long term.

a. 1990 Clean Air Act
b. 28-hour day
c. 33 Strategies of War
d. Financial statements

34. _________, when used as a special term, refers to various incentive plans introduced by businesses that provide direct or indirect payments to employees that depend on company's profitability in addition to employees' regular salary and bonuses. In publicly traded companies these plans typically amount to allocation of shares to employees.

The _________ plans are based on predetermined economic sharing rules that define the split of gains between the company as a principal and the employee as an agent.

a. Living wage
b. Wage
c. Federal Wage System
d. Profit sharing

35. In finance, an _________ is a contract between a buyer and a seller that gives the buyer the right--but not the obligation--to buy or to sell a particular asset (the underlying asset) at a later day at an agreed price. In return for granting the _________, the seller collects a payment (the premium) from the buyer. A call _________ gives the buyer the right to buy the underlying asset; a put _________ gives the buyer of the _________ the right to sell the underlying asset.
a. Option
b. A4e
c. AAAI
d. A Stake in the Outcome

36. A _________ is a compensation, usually financial, received by a worker in exchange for their labor.

Compensation in terms of _________s is given to worker and compensation in terms of salary is given to employees. Compensation is a monetary benefits given to employees in returns of the services provided by them.

a. Wage
b. Profit-sharing agreement
c. Performance-related pay
d. State Compensation Insurance Fund

37. In economics and sociology, an _________ is any factor (financial or non-financial) that enables or motivates a particular course of action, or counts as a reason for preferring one choice to the alternatives. It is an expectation that encourages people to behave in a certain way. Since human beings are purposeful creatures, the study of _________ structures is central to the study of all economic activity (both in terms of individual decision-making and in terms of co-operation and competition within a larger institutional structure.)
a. AAAI
b. Incentive
c. A Stake in the Outcome
d. A4e

38. An _________ is a formal scheme used to promote or encourage specific actions or behavior by a specific group of people during a defined period of time. _________s are particularly used in business management to motivate employees, and in sales in order to attract and retain customers. The scientific literature also refers to this concept as Pay for Performance.
a. AAAI
b. A Stake in the Outcome
c. A4e
d. Incentive program

1. A chief executive officer (_________) or chief executive is one of the highest-ranking corporate officer (executive) or administrator in charge of total management. An individual selected as President and _________ of a corporation, company, organization, or agency, reports to the board of directors. In internal communication and press releases, many companies capitalize the term and those of other high positions, even when they are not proper nouns.

a. Portfolio manager
b. Chief executive officer
c. Director of communications
d. CEO

2. _________ has been described as the 'process of social influence in which one person can enlist the aid and support of others in the accomplishment of a common task' . A definition more inclusive of followers comes from Alan Keith of Genentech who said '_________ is ultimately about creating a way for people to contribute to making something extraordinary happen.'

_________ is one of the most salient aspects of the organizational context. However, defining _________ has been challenging.

a. Leadership
b. 28-hour day
c. Situational leadership
d. 1990 Clean Air Act

3. _________ can be regarded as an outcome of mental processes (cognitive process) leading to the selection of a course of action among several alternatives. Every _________ process produces a final choice. The output can be an action or an opinion of choice.

a. Decision making
b. 33 Strategies of War
c. 1990 Clean Air Act
d. 28-hour day

4. _________ describes the situation when output from (or information about the result of) an event or phenomenon in the past will influence the same event/phenomenon in the present or future. When an event is part of a chain of cause-and-effect that forms a circuit or loop, then the event is said to 'feed back' into itself.

_________ is also a synonym for:

- _________ signal; the information about the initial event that is the basis for subsequent modification of the event.
- _________ loop; the causal path that leads from the initial generation of the _________ signal to the subsequent modification of the event.

_________ is a mechanism, process or signal that is looped back to control a system within itself. Such a loop is called a _________ loop.

a. Feedback
b. 1990 Clean Air Act
c. Feedback loop
d. Positive feedback

5. _________ is a term used to describe a policy of allowing events to take their own course. The term is a French phrase literally meaning 'let do'. It is a doctrine that states that government generally should not intervene in the marketplace.
a. Libertarian
b. Freedom of contract
c. Laissez-faire
d. Deep ecology

6. _________ is a civil designation for persons who are incorporated in a fixed or permanent way to a society or group: regular member of the working staff, permanent staff distinguished from a supernumerary.

The term '_________' and its counterpart, 'supernumerary,' originated in Spanish and Latin American academy and government; it is now also used in countries all over the world, such as France, the U.S., England, Italy, etc.

There are _________ members of surgical organizations, of universities, of gastronomical associations, etc.

a. Affiliation
b. Adam Smith
c. Abraham Harold Maslow
d. Numerary

7. The _________ captures an expanded spectrum of values and criteria for measuring organizational success: economic, ecological and social. With the ratification of the United Nations and ICLEI _________ standard for urban and community accounting in early 2007, this became the dominant approach to public sector full cost accounting. Similar UN standards apply to natural capital and human capital measurement to assist in measurements required by _________, e.g. the ecoBudget standard for reporting ecological footprint.

a. 1990 Clean Air Act
b. 33 Strategies of War
c. 28-hour day
d. Triple bottom line

8. _________ is a class of behavioural theory that claims that there is no best way to organize a corporation, to lead a company, or to make decisions. Instead, the optimal course of action is contingent (dependant) upon the internal and external situation. Several contingency approaches were developed concurrently in the late 1960s.
a. Commercial management
b. Distributed management
c. Capability management
d. Contingency theory

9. _________ is one of the managerial functions like planning, organizing, staffing and directing. It is an important function because it helps to check the errors and to take the corrective action so that deviation from standards are minimized and stated goals of the organization are achieved in desired manner.According to modern concepts, _________ is a foreseeing action whereas earlier concept of _________ was used only when errors were detected. _________ in management means setting standards, measuring actual performance and taking corrective action.
a. Turnover
b. Decision tree pruning
c. Schedule of reinforcement
d. Control

10. A _________ is a research instrument consisting of a series of questions and other prompts for the purpose of gathering information from respondents. Although they are often designed for statistical analysis of the responses, this is not always the case. The _________ was invented by Sir Francis Galton.
a. Questionnaire construction
b. Mystery shoppers
c. Structured interview
d. Questionnaire

11. _________ is the act by an employer of terminating employment. Though such a decision can be made by an employer for a variety of reasons, ranging from an economic downturn to performance-related problems on the part of the employee, being fired has a strong stigma in many cultures. To be fired, as opposed to quitting voluntarily (or being laid off), is often perceived as being the employee's fault, and is therefore considered to be disgraceful and a sign of failure.

a. Layoff
b. Severance package
c. Termination of employment
d. Firing

12. A _________ is a form of periodic payment from an employer to an employee, which may be specified in an employment contract. It is contrasted with piece wages, where each job, hour or other unit is paid separately, rather than on a periodic basis.

From the point of a view of running a business, _________ can also be viewed as the cost of acquiring human resources for running operations, and is then termed personnel expense or _________ expense.

a. Human resources
b. Salary
c. Human resource management
d. Training and development

13. The _________ is a leadership theory in the field of organizational studies developed by Robert House in 1971 and revised in 1996. The theory that a leader's behavior is contingent to the satisfaction, motivation and performance of subordinates. The revised version also argues that the leader engage in behaviors that complement subordinate's abilities and compensate for deficiencies.
a. Sociotechnical systems
b. Human relations
c. Corporate Culture
d. Path-goal theory

14. _________ is an organization's process of defining its strategy and making decisions on allocating its resources to pursue this strategy, including its capital and people. Various business analysis techniques can be used in _________, including SWOT analysis (Strengths, Weaknesses, Opportunities, and Threats) and PEST analysis (Political, Economic, Social, and Technological analysis) or STEER analysis involving Socio-cultural, Technological, Economic, Ecological, and Regulatory factors and EPISTEL (Environment, Political, Informatic, Social, Technological, Economic and Legal)

_________ is the formal consideration of an organization's future course. All _________ deals with at least one of three key questions:

1. 'What do we do?'
2. 'For whom do we do it?'
3. 'How do we excel?'

In business _________, the third question is better phrased 'How can we beat or avoid competition?'. (Bradford and Duncan, page 1.)

a. 28-hour day
b. Strategic planning
c. 33 Strategies of War
d. 1990 Clean Air Act

15. In game theory, an _________ is a set of moves or strategies taken by the players, or their payoffs resulting from the actions or strategies taken by all players. The two are complementary in that given knowledge of the set of strategies of all players, the final state of the game is known, as are any relevant payoffs. In a game where chance or a random event is involved, the _________ is not known from only the set of strategies, but is only realized when the random event(s) are realized.

a. Outcome
b. A4e
c. AAAI
d. A Stake in the Outcome

16. _________ is individual power based on a high level of identification with, admiration of, or respect for the powerholder.

Nationalism, Patriotism, Celebrities and well-respected people are examples of _________ in effect.

_________ is one of the Five Bases of Social Power, as defined by Bertram Raven and his colleagues[1] in 1959.

a. 28-hour day
b. 33 Strategies of War
c. 1990 Clean Air Act
d. Referent power

17. _________ 'is the use of one's individual or assigned power within an employing organization for the purpose of obtaining advantages beyond one's legitimate authority. Those advantages may include access to tangible assets, or intangible benefits such as status or pseudo-authority that influences the behavior of others. Both individuals and groups may engage in _________.'

_________ differs from office gossip in that people participating in _________ do so with the objective of gaining advantage, whereas gossip can be a purely social activity.

a. AAAI
b. A Stake in the Outcome
c. Office politics
d. A4e

18. _________ refers to increasing the spiritual, political, social or economic strength of individuals and communities. It often involves the empowered developing confidence in their own capacities.

The term Human _________ covers a vast landscape of meanings, interpretations, definitions and disciplines ranging from psychology and philosophy to the highly commercialized Self-Help industry and Motivational sciences.

a. A Stake in the Outcome
b. AAAI
c. A4e
d. Empowerment

1. _________ is one of the managerial functions like planning, organizing, staffing and directing. It is an important function because it helps to check the errors and to take the corrective action so that deviation from standards are minimized and stated goals of the organization are achieved in desired manner.According to modern concepts, _________ is a foreseeing action whereas earlier concept of _________ was used only when errors were detected. _________ in management means setting standards, measuring actual performance and taking corrective action.

   a. Schedule of reinforcement
   b. Turnover
   c. Decision tree pruning
   d. Control

2. 'Speaking generally, properties are those physical quantities which directly describe the physical attributes of the system; _________s are those combinations of the properties which suffice to determine the response of the system. Properties can have all sorts of dimensions, depending upon the system being considered; _________s are dimensionless, or have the dimension of time or its reciprocal.'

The term can also be used in engineering contexts, however, as it is typically used in the physical sciences.

When the terms formal _________ and actual _________ are used, they generally correspond with the definitions used in computer science.

   a. Parameter
   b. 33 Strategies of War
   c. 1990 Clean Air Act
   d. 28-hour day

3. A _________ is a change implemented to address a weakness identified in a management system. Normally _________s are implemented in response to a customer complaint, abnormal levels of internal nonconformity, nonconformities identified during an internal audit or adverse or unstable trends in product and process monitoring such as would be identified by SPC.

The process of determining a _________ requires identification of actions that can be taken to prevent or mitigate the weakness.

   a. Corrective action
   b. Zero defects
   c. 28-hour day
   d. 1990 Clean Air Act

4. _________ comprises the actual output or results of an organization as measured against its intended outputs (or goals and objectives.)

Specialists in many fields are concerned with _________ including strategic planners, operations, finance, legal, and organizational development.

In recent years, many organizations have attempted to manage _________ using the balanced scorecard methodology where performance is tracked and measured in multiple dimensions such as:

- financial performance (e.g. shareholder return)
- customer service
- social responsibility (e.g. corporate citizenship, community outreach)
- employee stewardship

.

a. AAAI
b. Organizational performance
c. A Stake in the Outcome
d. A4e

5. _________ is the concept of how effective an organization is in achieving the outcomes the organization intends to produce. The idea of _________ is especially important for non-profit organizations as most people who donate money to non-profit organizations and charities are interested in knowing whether the organization is effective in accomplishing its goals.

An organization's effectiveness is also dependent on its communicative competence and ethics.

a. Informal organization
b. Organizational structure
c. Organizational development
d. Organizational effectiveness

6. _________ refers to metrics and measures of output from production processes, per unit of input. Labor _________, for example, is typically measured as a ratio of output per labor-hour, an input. _________ may be conceived of as a metrics of the technical or engineering efficiency of production.

a. Master production schedule
b. Value engineering
c. Remanufacturing
d. Productivity

7. _________ is an advertisement in which a particular product specifically mentions a competitor by name for the express purpose of showing why the competitor is inferior to the product naming it.

This should not be confused with parody advertisements, where a fictional product is being advertised for the purpose of poking fun at the particular advertisement, nor should it be confused with the use of a coined brand name for the purpose of comparing the product without actually naming an actual competitor. ('Wikipedia tastes better and is less filling than the Encyclopedia Galactica.')

In the 1980s, during what has been referred to as the cola wars, soft-drink manufacturer Pepsi ran a series of advertisements where people, caught on hidden camera, in a blind taste test, chose Pepsi over rival Coca-Cola.

a. 33 Strategies of War
b. 28-hour day
c. 1990 Clean Air Act
d. Comparative advertising

8. The 'business case for _________', theorizes that in a global marketplace, a company that employs a diverse workforce (both men and women, people of many generations, people from ethnically and racially diverse backgrounds etc.) is better able to understand the demographics of the marketplace it serves and is thus better equipped to thrive in that marketplace than a company that has a more limited range of employee demographics.

An additional corollary suggests that a company that supports the _________ of its workforce can also improve employee satisfaction, productivity and retention.

a. Kanban
b. Trademark
c. Virtual team
d. Diversity

9. The _________ is the labour pool in employment. It is generally used to describe those working for a single company or industry, but can also apply to a geographic region like a city, country, state, etc. The term generally excludes the employers or management, and implies those involved in manual labour.
a. Division of labour
b. Workforce
c. Work-life balance
d. Pink-collar worker

10. _________ describes the situation when output from (or information about the result of) an event or phenomenon in the past will influence the same event/phenomenon in the present or future. When an event is part of a chain of cause-and-effect that forms a circuit or loop, then the event is said to 'feed back' into itself.

_________ is also a synonym for:

- _________ signal; the information about the initial event that is the basis for subsequent modification of the event.
- _________ loop; the causal path that leads from the initial generation of the _________ signal to the subsequent modification of the event.

_________ is a mechanism, process or signal that is looped back to control a system within itself. Such a loop is called a _________ loop.

a. Feedback loop
b. Positive feedback
c. 1990 Clean Air Act
d. Feedback

11. The _________ of 2002 (Pub.L. 107-204, 116 Stat. 745, enacted July 30, 2002), also known as the Public Company Accounting Reform and Investor Protection Act of 2002 and commonly called Sarbanes-Oxley, Sarbox or SOX, is a United States federal law enacted on July 30, 2002, as a reaction to a number of major corporate and accounting scandals including those affecting Enron, Tyco International, Adelphia, Peregrine Systems and WorldCom.
a. Sarbanes-Oxley Act
b. Letter of credit
c. Sarbanes-Oxley Act of 2002
d. Fair Labor Standards Act

12. A _________ is a subset of the overall internal controls of a business covering the application of people, documents, technologies, and procedures by management accountants to solving business problems such as costing a product, service or a business-wide strategy. _________s are distinct from regular information systems in that they are used to analyze other information systems applied in operational activities in the organization. Academically, the term is commonly used to refer to the group of information management methods tied to the automation or support of human decision making, e.g. Decision Support Systems, Expert systems, and Executive information systems.
a. Strategic information system
b. 1990 Clean Air Act
c. Management information system
d. 28-hour day

13. _________ is the process of comparing the cost, cycle time, productivity, or quality of a specific process or method to another that is widely considered to be an industry standard or best practice. Essentially, _________ provides a snapshot of the performance of your business and helps you understand where you are in relation to a particular standard. The result is often a business case for making changes in order to make improvements.

a. Cost leadership
b. Benchmarking
c. Competitive heterogeneity
d. Complementors

14. A _________ is the belief that there is a technique, method, process, activity, incentive or reward that is more effective at delivering a particular outcome than any other technique, method, process, etc. The idea is that with proper processes, checks, and testing, a desired outcome can be delivered with fewer problems and unforeseen complications. _________s can also be defined as the most efficient (least amount of effort) and effective (best results) way of accomplishing a task, based on repeatable procedures that have proven themselves over time for large numbers of people.
a. Hierarchical organization
b. Best practice
c. Fix it twice
d. Design management

15. Employees typically must relinquish some of their _________, but how much they must do so can be a contentious issue. Employers might choose to monitor employees activities using surveillance cameras, or may wish to record employees activities while using company owned computers or telephones.

The EU Directive 95/46/EC on the protection of individuals with regard to the processing of personal data and on the free movement of such data limits and regulates the collection of personal information on individuals, including workers.

a. Complement
b. Procter ' Gamble
c. Privacy while at the workplace
d. Job security through obscurity

16. _________ is unwelcome harassment of a sexual nature, or based upon the receiving party's sex or gender. In some contexts or circumstances, _________ may be illegal. It includes a range of behavior from seemingly mild transgressions and annoyances to actual sexual abuse or sexual assault.
a. 1990 Clean Air Act
b. Hypernorms
c. 28-hour day
d. Sexual harassment

17. _________ is a contract between two parties, one being the employer and the other being the employee. An employee may be defined as: 'A person in the service of another under any contract of hire, express or implied, oral or written, where the employer has the power or right to control and direct the employee in the material details of how the work is to be performed.' Black's Law Dictionary page 471 (5th ed. 1979.)

a. Employment rate
b. Employment
c. Exit interview
d. Employment counsellor

18. _________ is the set of processes, customs, policies, laws, and institutions affecting the way a corporation (or company) is directed, administered or controlled. _________ also includes the relationships among the many stakeholders involved and the goals for which the corporation is governed. The principal stakeholders are the shareholders/members, management, and the board of directors.

a. No-FEAR Act
b. Flextime
c. Guarantee
d. Corporate governance

1. _________ is an area of business concerned with the production of goods and services, and involves the responsibility of ensuring that business operations are efficient in terms of using as little resource as needed, and effective in terms of meeting customer requirements. It is concerned with managing the process that converts inputs (in the forms of materials, labour and energy) into outputs (in the form of goods and services.)

Operations traditionally refers to the production of goods and services separately, although the distinction between these two main types of operations is increasingly difficult to make as manufacturers tend to merge product and service offerings.

a. A4e
b. AAAI
c. Operations management
d. A Stake in the Outcome

2. _________ is one of the managerial functions like planning, organizing, staffing and directing. It is an important function because it helps to check the errors and to take the corrective action so that deviation from standards are minimized and stated goals of the organization are achieved in desired manner.According to modern concepts, _________ is a foreseeing action whereas earlier concept of _________ was used only when errors were detected. _________ in management means setting standards, measuring actual performance and taking corrective action.

a. Turnover
b. Decision tree pruning
c. Schedule of reinforcement
d. Control

3. _________ are goods that have completed the manufacturing process but have not yet been sold or distributed to the end user.

Manufacturing has three classes of inventory:

1. Raw material
2. Work in process
3. _________

A good purchased as a 'raw material' goes into the manufacture of a product. A good only partially completed during the manufacturing process is called 'work in process'. When the good is completed as to manufacturing but not yet sold or distributed to the end-user is called a 'finished good'.

a. 1990 Clean Air Act
b. 28-hour day
c. Reorder point
d. Finished goods

4. _________ is an advertisement in which a particular product specifically mentions a competitor by name for the express purpose of showing why the competitor is inferior to the product naming it.

This should not be confused with parody advertisements, where a fictional product is being advertised for the purpose of poking fun at the particular advertisement, nor should it be confused with the use of a coined brand name for the purpose of comparing the product without actually naming an actual competitor. ('Wikipedia tastes better and is less filling than the Encyclopedia Galactica.')

In the 1980s, during what has been referred to as the cola wars, soft-drink manufacturer Pepsi ran a series of advertisements where people, caught on hidden camera, in a blind taste test, chose Pepsi over rival Coca-Cola.

a. 1990 Clean Air Act
b. 33 Strategies of War
c. 28-hour day
d. Comparative advertising

5. _________ refers to metrics and measures of output from production processes, per unit of input. Labor _________, for example, is typically measured as a ratio of output per labor-hour, an input. _________ may be conceived of as a metrics of the technical or engineering efficiency of production.

a. Remanufacturing
b. Master production schedule
c. Value engineering
d. Productivity

6. _________ concern the operation of a facility, as opposed to maintenance, supply and distribution, health, and safety, emergency response, human resources, security, information technology and other infrastructural support organizations.

Personnel that make up 'operations' are

- operators
- engineers
- technicians
- management

This is mainly in a manufacturing setting.

a. Conglomerate merger
b. Labor intensive
c. Market niche
d. Manufacturing Operations

7. The _________ is a concept from business management that was first described and popularized by Michael Porter in his 1985 best-seller, Competitive Advantage: Creating and Sustaining Superior Performance.

A _________ is a chain of activities. Products pass through all activities of the chain in order and at each activity the product gains some value. The chain of activities gives the products more added value than the sum of added values of all activities. It is important not to mix the concept of the _________ with the costs occurring throughout the activities.

a. Market development
b. Mass marketing
c. Customer relationship management
d. Value chain

8. _________ are legal property rights over creations of the mind, both artistic and commercial, and the corresponding fields of law. Under _________ law, owners are granted certain exclusive rights to a variety of intangible assets, such as musical, literary, and artistic works; ideas, discoveries and inventions; and words, phrases, symbols, and designs. Common types of _________ include copyrights, trademarks, patents, industrial design rights and trade secrets.

a. Equal Pay Act
b. Unemployment Action Center
c. Intent
d. Intellectual property

9. _________ plant, and equipment, is a term used in accountancy for assets and property which cannot easily be converted into cash. This can be compared with current assets such as cash or bank accounts, which are described as liquid assets. In most cases, only tangible assets are referred to as fixed.

a. 1990 Clean Air Act
b. 33 Strategies of War
c. 28-hour day
d. Fixed asset

10. _________ is a business management strategy, initially implemented by Motorola, that today enjoys widespread application in many sectors of industry.

_________ seeks to improve the quality of process outputs by identifying and removing the causes of defects (errors) and variation in manufacturing and business processes. It uses a set of quality management methods, including statistical methods, and creates a special infrastructure of people within the organization ('Black Belts' etc.)

a. Production line
b. Takt time
c. Theory of constraints
d. Six Sigma

11. _________ can be considered to have three main components: quality control, quality assurance and quality improvement. _________ is focused not only on product quality, but also the means to achieve it. _________ therefore uses quality assurance and control of processes as well as products to achieve more consistent quality.
a. Total quality management
b. Quality management
c. 28-hour day
d. 1990 Clean Air Act

12. _________, in marketing, manufacturing, call centres and management, is the use of flexible computer-aided manufacturing systems to produce custom output. Those systems combine the low unit costs of mass production processes with the flexibility of individual customization.

'_________' is the new frontier in business competition for both manufacturing and service industries.

a. Mass customization
b. 33 Strategies of War
c. 1990 Clean Air Act
d. 28-hour day

13. _________ is a broad label that refers to any individuals or households that use goods and services generated within the economy. The concept of a _________ is used in different contexts, so that the usage and significance of the term may vary.

Typically when business people and economists talk of _________s they are talking about person as _________, an aggregated commodity item with little individuality other than that expressed in the buy/not-buy decision.

a. 28-hour day
b. 33 Strategies of War
c. 1990 Clean Air Act
d. Consumer

Chapter 1

1. d	2. d	3. c	4. a	5. d	6. d	7. d	8. a	9. d

Chapter 2

1. d	2. c	3. d	4. c	5. d	6. a	7. d	8. d	9. d	10. d
11. d	12. a	13. c	14. d	15. d	16. d	17. a	18. d	19. b	20. d
21. d	22. a	23. d	24. b	25. b					

Chapter 3

1. d	2. b	3. b	4. a	5. a	6. b	7. d	8. a	9. c	10. d
11. d	12. a	13. d	14. a						

Chapter 4

1. d	2. b	3. a	4. d	5. b	6. a	7. a	8. d	9. d	10. b
11. d	12. c	13. c	14. d	15. d	16. d	17. d	18. a	19. d	20. a
21. d	22. c	23. d	24. d						

Chapter 5

1. c	2. d	3. d	4. d	5. a	6. d	7. d	8. a	9. a	10. d
11. b	12. c	13. d	14. d	15. d	16. b	17. d	18. b		

Chapter 6

1. d	2. b	3. c	4. d	5. d	6. c	7. d	8. c	9. d	10. b
11. a	12. c	13. a	14. c	15. a	16. c	17. d	18. a	19. d	20. b
21. d	22. b								

Chapter 7

1. d	2. c	3. c	4. d	5. d	6. d

Chapter 8

1. a	2. a	3. a	4. c	5. b	6. c	7. d	8. d	9. d	10. c
11. d	12. d	13. d	14. a	15. a	16. c	17. d	18. d	19. d	20. b
21. d	22. d	23. d	24. d	25. d	26. b	27. c	28. d	29. d	30. d
31. a	32. a								

Chapter 9

1. d	2. d	3. d	4. a	5. a	6. d	7. d	8. d	9. c	10. d
11. b	12. d	13. d	14. d	15. a	16. d	17. c	18. d	19. b	20. d
21. b	22. d	23. a	24. d						

Chapter 10

1. b	2. d	3. d	4. d	5. d	6. b	7. c	8. d	9. d	10. d
11. d	12. a	13. c	14. a	15. a	16. d	17. c	18. d	19. c	20. c
21. a	22. d	23. c							

Chapter 11

1. d	2. a	3. c	4. c	5. d	6. a	7. c	8. d	9. c	10. d
11. b	12. b	13. c	14. c	15. d	16. d	17. d	18. d		

Chapter 12

1. c	2. d	3. d	4. d	5. b	6. d	7. c	8. d	9. b	10. d
11. c	12. c	13. b	14. d	15. d	16. b	17. d	18. d	19. d	20. d
21. d	22. b	23. d	24. d	25. d	26. d	27. d	28. b	29. a	30. d
31. d	32. c	33. d							

Chapter 13

1. d	2. d	3. b	4. d	5. c	6. b	7. b	8. b	9. d

Chapter 14

1. d	2. d	3. d	4. d	5. d	6. a	7. a	8. a	9. a	10. d
11. d	12. d	13. c	14. a	15. d	16. d	17. a	18. d	19. c	20. c
21. d	22. d	23. d	24. d	25. d	26. d	27. c	28. a		

Chapter 15

1. a	2. b	3. a	4. d	5. d	6. d	7. c	8. d	9. a	10. b
11. d	12. d	13. c	14. a	15. b	16. d	17. a			

Chapter 16

1. c	2. b	3. d	4. d	5. d	6. b	7. d	8. c	9. d	10. b
11. c	12. a	13. d	14. d	15. b	16. c	17. a	18. d	19. a	20. a
21. a	22. d	23. d	24. d	25. c	26. d	27. d	28. d	29. a	30. d
31. c	32. b	33. d	34. d	35. a	36. a	37. b	38. d		

Chapter 17

1. d	2. a	3. a	4. a	5. c	6. d	7. d	8. d	9. d	10. d
11. d	12. b	13. d	14. b	15. a	16. d	17. c	18. d		

Chapter 18

1. d	2. a	3. a	4. b	5. d	6. d	7. d	8. d	9. b	10. d
11. a	12. c	13. b	14. b	15. c	16. d	17. b	18. d		

Chapter 19

1. c	2. d	3. d	4. d	5. d	6. d	7. d	8. d	9. d	10. d
11. b	12. a	13. d							

www.ingramcontent.com/pod-product-compliance
Lightning Source LLC
Chambersburg PA
CBHW082045230426
43670CB00016B/2785
* 9 7 8 1 4 2 8 8 7 2 6 1 5 *